Joey —

Here's to a
wonderful new friendship!

I can't wait to write
about your booze
business venture.

All the best —

Arthur

INSIDE THE BOTTLE

PEOPLE, BRANDS, AND STORIES

ARTHUR SHAPIRO

AM SHAPIRO & ASSOCIATES LLC

A|M Shapiro & Associates LLC

A|M Shapiro & Associates, LLC
515 East 79th Street #11B
New York, NY 10075

www.boozebusiness.com

ISBN-10: 0-9976181-0-8
ISBN-13: 978-0-9976181-0-5

First Edition

Printed in the United States of America

Produced by Hannah Forman

Cover Design, Illustrations, Layout, and Index by Miki Hickel

TABLE OF CONTENTS

Introduction

Like most business people and many consumers, I've always been captivated by image and fashion businesses. Businesses where the 'product' is largely based on perception or imagery—how it makes you look or feel, more than the efficacy of the product itself. Like cosmetics and fragrances, for the alcohol industry, what's in the bottle is generally secondary to the statement the brand makes when you order, buy, and use it. Until recently, that is.

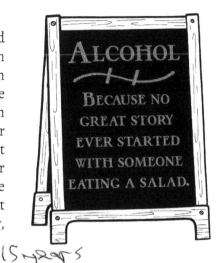

My 30 years' experience in the alcohol industry can be summed up in two phases: as a senior executive at the Seagram Spirits and Wine Company, and later as a consultant to a wide range of businesses in the industry.

Until its demise, the Seagram Spirits and Wine Company was the leader in the spirits (liquor) industry in the U.S. For 50 years, the company set the pace and tone for the marketing of products and building brands. From the 1980's to the end of the century (and the end of the company), Seagram brands—such as Chivas Regal, Crown Royal, Absolut, Captain Morgan, Seagram 7, and others—grew and flourished, despite the obstacles imposed on the marketing of liquor brands, and in the face of stiff competition.

From 1986 to 2001, I had a front-row seat, working in senior marketing positions primarily in the U.S., but also in Asia-Pacific and Latin America. The jobs ranged from market research to marketing services, new products, and ultimately, chief marketing officer for the Americas.

Seagram was a company of stories, and *Inside the Bottle* tells these stories and provides insights into consumer marketing in the alcohol industry. But this book is about more than just business and marketing; it is a firsthand account of the closing history of a once-great company. *Inside the Bottle* seeks to entertain readers—both marketers and consumers alike—with anecdotes and myth-shattering truths about the liquor business and its brand-building escapades.

After Seagram, I started a consulting practice, working with the major spirits companies on a wide range of business and marketing projects. Over time, the practice shifted toward startup ventures, which are generally more exciting and fun than working for the "suits."

Let me illustrate the point. Not long ago, a major spirits company hired me to assist in the development of a global strategy for American Whiskey. I was on a Skype call at 4:00 a.m. ET with managers from all over the world, discussing needs and wants, preferences and tastes, strategic issues, tactics, experiences, and the like. Suddenly it hit me: of the six managers on the call, I guessed that three of them would be in different jobs in five years or less, and the remaining three would no longer be with the company. So I asked myself: what the hell am I doing up in the middle of the night discussing a topic that will become irrelevant to all of us? At that moment, I decided that the **Booze Business** is fun and fascinating, and that I would become an observer, a reporter, and an advisor to startups, rather than a consultant to the large companies.

And so, the blog boozebusiness.com was born, and this journey began.

The spirits and wine industry is intriguing. I've been in and around it for much of my work life, and even though my general consulting work has taken me to other industries, the Booze Business continues to fascinate me.

It's an industry that, despite its size and growth, is small. It's a business of people, relationships, and stories. Lots of stories.

It is also an industry that has undergone significant changes in the 30 years I have been a part of it. Consider this:

- The industry has consolidated at all levels: manufacturer (supplier), distributor, and retailer.

- Consumer preferences have moved from whiskies to vodka and back to whiskies. Purchase motivations have gone from strictly imagery and marketing hype, to "how is it made?" and "what's in the bottle?"

- Mass-produced brands are losing ground to craft and micro distillers.

At no point in the 80 plus years since the end of Prohibition has there been as much turmoil as we've seen in the last 30. This is my attempt to capture the turbulence, examine it, and laugh about it.

While the stories, the people, business principles, and brand-building concepts center on the alcohol industry, the lessons learned are applicable to a wide range of businesses. Especially businesses in which imagery plays an important role; businesses in which consumer preferences rule the balance sheet; where marketing and sales need to be on the same page; and businesses wherein the difference between winning and losing is the balance between innovation and risk-taking.

Finally, from the outset of this journey, I have hoped that my readers would include the people across the bar and on the other side of the bottle— the consumers who imbibe and enjoy. Hopefully this book will shed some light on a fascinating industry that few outside it know much about.

*   *   *

About this book

This book is based on a compilation of some of my blog postings over the last 5 years, from nearly 300 postings and articles. In some instances, I've edited them to bring them up to date, add a nuance, or amplify the story. In addition to organizing the posts into thematic and relevant chapters, I've provided a context and frame of reference. So while this book stems from the Booze Business blog postings since 2010, it also presents stories and ideas beyond the blog.

1. Booze—Tonic or Toxic?

When I first came to the alcohol industry in the mid-80s, I was struck by the formality and protocol of the industry in general, and Seagram in particular. One did not use the term "alcoholic beverage," but used "beverage alcohol" instead. No really—it pissed people off if you used the former, I suppose because it reminded the industry that there are abusers out there. But if you said "beverage alcohol," poof, no drunks.

The taboo that I found very amusing was the prohibition (pun intended) on the use of the word "booze." Never mind that everyone uses that expression; a proper gentleman in the drinks business did not use any terms or expressions that could convey a sense of impropriety. So never call it booze, I was told.

Ha. It's the **Booze Business**. Get over it. It's not pejorative; it's slang.

Two thoughts about the industry come immediately to mind. The first is that in the U.S., the alcohol industry carries a bit of a stigma—not as bad as the tobacco industry, but still considered a "sin" business to some. Americans think of bootleggers, moonshiners, and other, shall we say, outside-the-mainstream businesspeople that want them to get drunk and entice their children into the vices of "demon rum." Contrast that with the view of the industry in the U.K.; there the industry is referred to as the "Drinks Business," and the purveyors and industry leaders are sometimes knighted or receive the Order of the British Empire (OBE). The differences in culture and history have resulted in different values.

The second thought that comes to mind is that the alcohol industry, thanks to the dark period known as prohibition, is sensitive about appearances and the use of language. I cannot tell you how many times I heard Seagram's in-house legal counsel kill an ad or piece of communication because it *could* be seen as improper. Their favorite expression was "the *appearance* of impropriety is as damaging as the impropriety itself."

For decades, most people thought there was a law against broadcast advertising (Radio and TV) for liquor, when in fact, it was a voluntary ban. After the repeal of prohibition, industry leaders were so afraid the "noble experiment" would come back, that they developed a bunker mentality, and decided not to stand out or engender any negative publicity. (As you'll see in Chapter 11, I was front and center in leading the charge to end this ban. It's an interesting story, and a good case study in marketing and public policy.)

Anyhow, I digress. Let's look at some thoughts on the basic aspects of the alcoholic beverage industry. Uh, I mean **Booze Business**.

✻   ✻   ✻

Why is it called Booze?

There are many definitions of the word "booze," and thoughts on how the term originated.

The *Merriam-Webster Dictionary* defines booze as "to drink a lot of alcohol." The *New Oxford American Dictionary* adds, "especially hard liquor."

The most common origin ascribes the word to either the Dutch or German word *būsen,* 'to drink to excess' or 'to carouse.' The spelling *booze* dates from the 18th century.

One of my favorite legends about the word booze is based on a promoter who promised free beer to anyone who came to one of his events. His name? Mr. Booz.

Another persistent myth traces the word to another Mr. Booz, a mid-19th century distiller from the Philadelphia area. Some say it comes from the Middle English word (circa 1300) *bouse,* meaning 'to drink.'

The story that makes the most sense to me (and didn't come from Google) is that the word's origin goes back to World War I and a contingent of "doughboys," the nickname given to the American Expeditionary Force that took part in the war. These troops were in a southwestern French town with no alcohol to consume, except for the local wine. The town was Buzet (pronounced "bu-zay")... as in Buzet Wine...as in "what's this here booze?"

Tonic or Toxic?

The late Bill Roesing, political and corporate strategist and former head of Seagram's Washington D.C. office, once described America as having a love-hate relationship with alcohol. He characterized U.S. history as consisting of tonic and toxic periods.

From the birth of the nation to the mid-1800s, alcohol was seen as a tonic. Think about the traveling "doctors" (a.k.a. snake oil salesmen) selling their alcohol-laced elixirs. Among other positive perceptions, alcohol was seen as "good for what ails you" and helping you to remain "healthy."

After the Civil War, for the next 60 years or so alcohol was considered toxic, culminating in the temperance movement and ultimately, Prohibition from 1920 to 1933.

In fact, during WWI, British soldiers were rationed two ounces of rum or a pint of porter daily. Germans received a pint of beer, half a pint of wine and a quarter pint of spirits. Canadians got shipments of Jamaican rum. But U.S. soldiers, under Prohibition laws, observed a "dry" zone around its bases.

By WWII, alcohol was widely available to our G.I.'s, and the tonic era began anew.

The tonic period has gotten stronger, thanks to 60 Minutes. A 1991 segment called the "French Paradox," described the benefits of red wine and has since extended to all alcohol. Today, many health authorities and experts see moderate consumption as beneficial.

Oh, by the way, for some interesting historical trends on alcohol, wine, and beer consumption, check out the most recent information from the Gallup people. They've been tracking drinking patterns in the U.S. since the late 1930s. The proportion of the U.S. population that drinks any alcohol product hasn't changed much since the late 1940s. (The chart has been updated and reflects 2015 data).

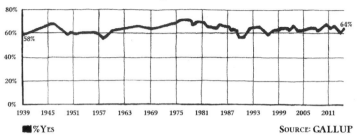

How small is the market?

I'm always struck by the size of the spirits category and small number of dedicated drinkers of a particular brand.

Let's do some math:

- The U.S. population over 21 is around 200 million.

- 60% of those over 21 drink alcohol at least occasionally, so 120 million people.

- People who drink spirits most often (as opposed to wine or beer) are about 20% of those who drink alcohol. So now we're down to 24 *million spirits drinkers.*

(Actually, the overall number who drink spirits is much higher; perhaps 80% of alcohol drinkers or close to 100 million. But I'm focusing on most often, the core of the market.)

The size of the core market at 24 million people can be seen as huge or small, depending on your perspective.

If half these drinkers consume vodka, that's 12 million people. But if a brand has a 25% share, the size of the "franchise" is only 3 million consumers. (The numbers get smaller as you get into different categories, like Cognac.)

In place of mass media, marketers need to think in terms of precision and targeting using, "a rifle, not a shotgun." Maybe even with a telescopic lens.

Whether aiming at increasing brand loyalty or converting users of competitive brands, it's all about the return on investment. Efforts such as relationship building programs, digital marketing, social media, database marketing, and point of sale programs, all are more effective than broad-brush mass media.

Just like the old expression "fish where the fish are"... but with a rod and reel, not a net.

*   *   *

I wrote this post five years ago, and it staggers me that many marketers, five years later, just don't seem to "get it," and fail to see the power of social media.

Here's an interesting view that Bryan Fey, president and CEO of Pernod Ricard USA had to say at the Shanken Impact Seminar in 2014, as reported by Shanken News Daily:

> *"Wine and spirits marketers also have been energetic in utilizing digital media to boost their brands... [He] told the Seminar audience that the industry is moving from 'spray and pray' marketing to a focus on the 'speed of the feed.' Traditional TV, print and outdoor executions, he said, must integrate into the brand stories being told online. Illustrating digital's power to reach legions of consumers worldwide, Fry pointed out that a $13,000 billboard spend garners around 320,000 impressions, while the same spend on social media can reach more than 6 million consumers. Digital formats also allow drinks companies to move beyond traditional brand pitches and hone in on service, which can be crucial in sectors like spirits, which consumers often find confusing to shop.*

The bar itself isn't about to go virtual, Fry added, but, especially for the younger generation, bar-goers' phones—and the digital access they provide—are rarely more than 30 centimeters from their drinks."

✻ ✻ ✻

How old is alcohol?

In an issue of Mark Brown's Industry News Update, there is a reprint of a *Wall Street Journal* article titled, "Perhaps a Red, 4100 B.C." Here's the story lead:

Scientists have discovered the world's oldest known winery, secreted amid dozens of prehistoric graves in a cavern in Armenia...

Outside a mountain village still known for its wine-making skill, archaeologists unearthed a large vat set in a platform for treading grapes, along with the well-preserved remains of crushed grapes, seeds and vine leaves, dating to about 6,100 years ago—a thousand years older than other comparable finds.

The article ends by providing a "prehistory" of wine, and indicates archaeologists have found traces of a fermented rice wine from a village in northern China dating back 9,000 years. Wow—alcohol use goes back 9,000 years!

But wait, there's more.

Last month, the newsletter reprinted an article from the *LA Times* called "Prohibition, online." The opening paragraph: "In most states, ordering a gun online is perfectly legal. As is ordering pornography, cigarettes and ammunition. A bottle of merlot, though, could land you in jail."

So tell me, where do Neanderthals come from?

Do different types of liquor have different effects on you?

Let's start with a basic premise: there are people who are allergic to alcohol. There are people who are allergic to any type of alcohol, and many who are physiologically affected by different types—people who avoid wine, for example. I even know someone who cannot drink wine and drinks only a particular brand of gin. But in this posting, I'm thinking about those drinkers in the mainstream who report an aversion based on the "drinking experience" or "the morning after."

I've been researching this topic lately, and have been thinking about it ever since I got into the **Booze Business**.

When you ask consumers about their alcohol preferences, many have clear-cut answers such as, "tequila makes me crazy," "whiskey makes me angry," "gin makes me sad, must be the junipers." My favorite is, "I'm allergic to tequila. Last time I drank it, I broke out in handcuffs."

Whether in focus groups or with friends, these beliefs are strongly held and generally tied back to a memorable occasion (perhaps forgettable occasion is a more accurate description). Usually, it's based on a particular episode of, ahem, being over-served or the maiden drinking voyage. But misconceptions play a big role; there is nothing in juniper to lead to sadness, and even if there were, the distillation process would eliminate it. Similarly, the agave plant from which mescal is distilled (tequila is a type of mescal) has nothing to do with mescaline.

Sorry folks, alcohol is alcohol. The differences one experiences from different types of liquor (and alcohol in general), in my opinion, have little or nothing to do with the liquor itself. There are many other factors at work.

What about the congeners (the substance produced during fermentation of alcoholic beverages)? While red wine and dark spirits have the greatest amount, they are present to different degrees in white (clear) spirits. They are also more responsible for the morning after than getting you to slur, "I love you man" during an evening's indulgence.

How about the mixers used as a possible explanation for the difference? Tequila is consumed as a shot half the time, and with sugar-laden margarita mixers the other half—do these play a role? Rum mixed with juices, sugar, or cola can affect the impact. Maybe it's the tonic in your G&T.

I think the culprit is the mood, occasion, and situation you are in while drinking. If you're planning to get hammered, or the situation calls for it, you will. If it's been a tough day and you're looking to unwind and mellow, what you choose to drink will have that result.

So in effect, it's in your mind rather than in your glass or bottle.

Here's something that sums it up. I found it on io9, a blog by *Gawker Media*:

...The question of whether mixers or congeners affect our experiences with different alcohols seems almost inconsequential; if you wholeheartedly believe that a tequila is your one way ticket to Bedlam, there's probably not a whole lot that can be said to convince you—or your body—otherwise.

Sounds right to me.

*　　*　　*

How the **Booze Business** intoxicated me

I never blogged about how I got to Seagram and the alcohol industry. Unlike most of my coworkers, when I joined, I came to the **Booze Business** in mid-career. It was not unusual to meet someone at Seagram who was, let's say, 45 years old, and had been there since graduating college. That phenomenon had a mixed effect. It created some inbreeding, but also fostered a sense of camaraderie and "the Seagram way of doing things." It also nurtured a sense of "us and them" vis-à-vis the workers/management and the owners, also known as the family. I will deal with that at length in the next chapter.

For now, I'd like to tell you a story about how I got there.

Before I came to Seagram, I had a robust career as a market researcher and marketing consultant at important firms including Yankelovich, Skelly and White, where at one point I ran the consumer research and consulting practice. The entrepreneurial bug bit, I went out on my own with some partners—and the venture failed. Such is life. While licking my wounds at a well-known but second-rate research and polling company, a headhunter recruited me for the position of Vice President, Marketing Research at Seagram. I was thrilled. Instead of being a seller/provider of research information, I was to become a buyer (and ultimately, a user). I thought I breezed through the interviews. Nailed it, as they say.

Nothing happened. Weeks turned to months, and interview after interview came and went, but no offer and no rejection. Florence Skelly, my boss and mentor in the research world, used to say that a "no" was the next best thing to a "yes." A "maybe" or nothing just left you hanging. And that's what they did.

Finally, having given up hope six months after the process began, the headhunter called to tell me that the new CEO, Edgar Bronfman Jr., would like to see me. My protests were swept away when she also said that this was it—make or break. I got ready for the interview.

I hate to show my age, but this was before the Internet and having the world at your fingertips. To learn about Bronfman and the company, I spent hours at the library searching for a nugget that would be impressive and close the deal. I can't remember which magazine article I found, just the *Eureka!* moment. It turned out that Mr. Bronfman (Edgar Jr., as we referred to him), had produced a film called The Border, starring Jack Nicholson, Harvey Keitel, and Valerie Perrine. The reviews were awful and the film flopped. I read somewhere that among the film's problems was the fact that they used market research in the form of consumer focus groups to help decide on the ending.

The day of the interview arrived, and as I waited (while sweating profusely), I decided how I was going to make my mark. I was ushered into Bronfman's office, and he made me relax immediately; he's a very nice and charming guy. We talked about the usual interview stuff, and I decided to tell him my philosophy of market research—its strengths and weaknesses.

"Mr. Bronfman," I began. "I believe that research is best when used as a descriptive tool, not a predictive one. People can tell you what they've done with a fair amount of accuracy, but almost always falter when telling you what they will do." He seemed to pay close attention, so I pressed on, and told him a true story about research and filmmaking.

"I worked with someone who was a pretty good market researcher in the consumer packaged goods area, but his ego got the better of him. He went off to Hollywood to conduct market research for a studio. He sold himself on his ability to predict what films will be successful and how to use his research for marketing spending. Presumably, a potential hit would be strenuously backed, while a potential failure would be shelved. He came to studio management one day and told them that their new multimillion-dollar film was doomed to failure, based on his research findings. Do you know what the film was, Mr. Bronfman?" Taking the bait, he said "no." "It was Star Wars," I replied. "He was using his knowledge of how to predict the reaction to a new laundry detergent to forecast the success or failure of a film."

"When can you start?" was his reply.

These words changed my life.

Marketing research is like a lamppost; some people lean on it and some people are illuminated by it.

2. Those Seagram Folks—Owners and Toilers

By the time I arrived at Seagram in 1986, I had missed the first act of the Seagram/Bronfman saga; but as fate would have it, I was there for the drama and the finale. Before the fall, it was a special place—not the largest in the business, but arguably the most important. Seagram set the pace and tone for the industry; what Seagram did, others followed. To this day, many in the industry—Seagram alums or not—will tell you that the industry changed when Seagram closed, and not for the better.

That specialness was a product of the Bronfman family and the influence of their values and beliefs. It was also a function of the people who worked there. Perhaps it was the "home-grown" and long-tenured employees; perhaps it was the "us vs. them" phenomenon; whatever, there was an esprit de corps among us toilers in the vineyard that set us apart from the rest of the industry. Many of the movers and shakers in the industry came from Seagram—and still do, to this day.

Let's take a look at this special place from two viewpoints: the family and the employees.

*   *   *

The Family – a.k.a. The Owners

So that we're all starting at the same place, a brief recap of the Seagram owners and their tale is in order.

Let's start with the cast of characters. Samuel Bronfman (known as Mr. Sam) was the founder of the company and patriarch of the family. Of his two sons, Edgar M. Bronfman (known as Edgar Sr. and to us toilers, the Chairman) ran the worldwide spirits and wine business, and was also the President of the World Jewish Congress. His other son Charles is a successful businessman and philanthropist. Edgar Sr.'s son Edgar Bronfman Jr. (known as Edgar and among the toilers, Junior) ran Seagram during the time I was there. His brother, Sam Bronfman II, ran the wine business.

In his review of the book *The Bronfmans* by Nicholas Faith, Frank J. Prial of the *New York Times* wrote on June 25, 2006:

> *With the possible exception of Robert Mondavi and his truculent offspring, no family in the wine and spirits world has attracted more attention over the years than the Bronfmans, the Canadian founders of the Seagram liquor empire. From Prohibition, when their illegal booze slaked our national thirst, to the 1990's, when the lure of show business and Hollywood caused them to lose both Seagram and a vast fortune, the Bronfmans were rarely out of the press. Their immense wealth, their shame over their bootlegger reputation, and their unrelenting quest for social status and corporate respectability, abetted by legions of flacks, made them irresistible targets in the financial pages and the gossip columns.*

> *Briefly, what happened was this: In 1995, Edgar Jr., eager to be a player in films and electronic media, sold Seagram's 25 percent stake in DuPont to buy MCA/Universal and Polygram Records for $15 billion — "with dubious results," as Faith says. Then, in 2000, he sold what had become Seagram-Universal to Vivendi, a French group led by "the magnetic megalomaniac" Jean-Marie Messier who, Faith writes, "destroyed the Seagram Empire, resulting in one of the biggest losses ever sustained by a single family." When Mr. Sam was alive, he would badger his children with the old adage "Shirt sleeves to shirt sleeves in three generations."*

There were a number of prominent expressions heard often at Seagram. One was "The Lucky Sperm Club"—success as an accident of birth. The first time I heard the expression was at a lunch in Dallas. Around the table were several of us from Seagram, a successful retailer who'd grown his small store into one of the largest in the market, and one of our distributors. This distributor was now lackadaisically running the business his father had built for their family. During the course of the lunch, the distributor's son was pontificating more than he should have been, and voiced some ridiculous opinions. At one point, the retailer looked at him and said, "What the hell do you know about that? You're just a lucky sperm. In fact, I think you're the chairman of the lucky sperm club."

The other expression was "Shirtsleeves to Shirtsleeves in Three Generations," (the Italian expression is "stables to stars to stables again.") In other words, the first generation builds, the second expands, and the third destroys. Let's start there.

*   *   *

Shirtsleeves to shirtsleeves

The Bronfman family changed the face of the Booze Business in America. Mr. Sam (Samuel Bronfman, the patriarch)—regardless of what he did or did not do during prohibition—was smart enough when it ended to hold off shipping goods until they aged, had great taste, and would command a premium price.

In his grandson's office (that would be Edgar Bronfman Jr.), there was a photo of Mr. Sam with the caption, "shirtsleeves to shirtsleeves in three generations." In a biography on Arts & Entertainment TV (A&E), Edgar Jr. looked into the camera and said earnestly, "not on my watch."

Not long after, at the turn of the century, he sold his birthright for a song.

No worries; the family holdings must have gone from $8 billion to $3 billion, I suppose. But, still a boatload of money.

Not quite shirtsleeves, but prophetic nonetheless.

The Bronfman Enigma

There had been lots of conversations among Seagram alumni since it was announced on January 21, 2011 that Edgar Bronfman Jr. was convicted of insider trading in a French court.

The news reports I read at the time raised a number of questions. According to *Crain's NY Business*, "The conviction came even though the prosecutor had recommended acquittal..." That's curious.

The report went on to say that "the prosecutor felt the executives did not have enough information themselves about the company's health." What? Are we talking Edgar Jr. here? Didn't have enough information after having bet the heritage and fortune on a guy who referred to himself as Master of the Universe? [Note: Jean-Marie Messier was frequently referred to by the nickname "J2M" based on his initials, or J6M (Jean-Marie Messier Moi-Meme-Maitre-du-Monde), which translates to Jean-Marie Messier: Myself Master of the World.]

Edgar Jr. sometimes referred to the ease and depth with which people in Hollywood were capable of lying. He described studio executives as people who can swear on their mother's life that it is raining outside; when both of you know it's a beautiful sunny day. Yet he couldn't wait to do business there.

Every year since the 1950s, Seagram ran the Seagram Family Association (SFA) meeting, an annual session for distributor principals and their senior managers. At what turned out to be the last SFA (though that wasn't known at the time), the deal to sell the company was in the works. Rumors were widespread, and felt to have a ring of truth. Every conversation among distributors and Seagram management alike dealt with the speculation. Junior was at the event, but hardly visible, staying in his suite the entire time—and based on subsequent occurrences—probably cutting the deals.

He showed up at the last session, where customarily the owner addressed the distributors to remind them that Seagram was a family in both the literal and figurative sense of the word, and to provide remarks on the state of the business and the future.

When he walked into the back of the room, he stopped and asked those of us running the session what we thought he should touch on in his remarks. What was the tempo, what were the top issues, what's on their minds?

The answer was candid. "What's on everyone's mind is—are we going to be sold?" "The concerns are palpable...they, we, all want to know what's going on."

He just looked at us and went onto the stage. Immediately, he began to address the topic of a sale in no uncertain terms. He said emphatically and repeatedly that Seagram was not for sale. It was almost as though he swore on his grandfather's grave that would not happen. Less than a month later, the announcement of a sale was made.

It was a sunny, beautiful day in southern California, but inside the meeting room, the rain was pouring down.

The saddest part is that Edgar Jr. orchestrated the end of his family's spirits and wine business in favor of the idea of integrating media, entertainment, information, and communications in one handheld device: the Smartphone. The idea he had was ahead of its time and with the wrong people.

New product failures I have known – Old Breed

When I think about new products that failed when I was at Seagram, Old Breed comes most readily to mind.

When I arrived at Seagram, the product was in a few markets, and it was failing miserably. The premise was interesting; Edgar Jr., aware of "shot and a beer" consumption, decided that a beer-flavored whiskey was a good idea, and pushed for it.

I suppose that the equivalency issue also had a role to play. Here's how the Distilled Spirits Council of the U.S. (DISCUS) defines the issue:

> *Alcohol is alcohol. A standard drink of regular beer (12 ounces), distilled spirits (1.5 ounces of 80-proof spirits) and wine (5 ounces) each contains the same amount of alcohol.*

> *This scientific fact, known as "alcohol equivalence," is a critical aspect of responsible drinking recognized by the leading federal departments on alcohol and health matters, state driver's manuals, and groups such as Mothers Against Drunk Driving.*

A blurring of the lines between beer and spirits sort of makes them equivalent from a product standpoint, and goes against the lack of equivalency in excise taxes.

In addition, a beer-flavored whiskey was seen as a novel new product idea.

The product failed on all counts. Wanting a shot of whiskey with a beer chaser is not the same as a whiskey that tastes like beer. There are expectations about the taste of a shot with a beer that can't be met with a bottled version. Even if the product tasted great, it can't replicate the fresh type—much less with a product that tasted like stale beer.

Everyone knew this, I learned upon arrival, but no one wanted to tell the emperor that his baby was ugly (to mix metaphors).

So the product limped along until one of my trade researchers interviewed a retailer who went ballistic when asked about Old Breed. "Tell them to get that crap out of here," he said.

What I love about market research is that being politically correct has little to no role in providing information, if done properly. As a result, the owner learned what the management team was loath to tell him. The product was pulled from the shelves the next day.

Lessons learned:

- To succeed, a new product has to be both unique and relevant.

- Concepts and premises can be brilliant, but the product must deliver. What's in the bottle has to meet expectations.

- A management team unable to speak candidly will not succeed.

- A corporate culture that creates an environment that punishes the messenger is doomed to failure.

*　　*　　*

Update:

The idea of mixing liquor and beer in the same bottle has come back, but the other way around. MillerCoors introduced a bourbon-flavored beer called Miller Fortune in 2014, and today there are a number of beers that are aged in whiskey and bourbon barrels. When Seagram launched Old Breed, it was partly due to the loss of whiskey occasions and sales to beer. Today, it's the brewer's turn to stem the tide of sales losses to spirits. The jury is still out.

*　　*　　*

Chivas Gin?

No, there's no such thing. But the idea almost got me fired.

When I ran new products at Seagram, filling gaps in the portfolio was a top item on the agenda. We needed a strong tequila entry, a vodka for sure, and an imported gin product.

Oh sure, we had the top seller in domestic gin (Seagram's Gin), but with the exception of Boodles, we did not have an imported brand to compete with Beefeater's, Tanqueray, or Bombay, among others.

Our research revealed that a strong overlap in preferences existed among scotch and gin drinkers. A scotch drinker was more likely to drink gin as a second choice, and vice versa.

Based on this insight and lots of concept development work, my friend Sam Ellias recommended a Chivas Gin. Before I could say a word, he quickly added that it would *not* be Chivas Regal Gin, but rather, a gin *from* Chivas Brothers. The brand would use the Chivas heritage of distilling expertise and skill, and apply it to a "white goods" product (industry speak for a clear product such as vodka or gin). Furthermore, his research showed that attitudes toward Chivas Regal Scotch improved as a result of the more contemporary gin brand idea. Trust me; at that time, Chivas Regal needed all the help it could get.

I was convinced.

At the next new products review meeting, we put the idea on the table for discussion and approval to proceed to the next development stage. There was strong support, but something wasn't right. Those in the room with doctorate degrees in "Owner Anger Detection" (OAD) became uneasy. I couldn't understand it, but knew enough to drop the subject based on instinct.

But not Sam Ellias.

A number of years later, when I was running marketing and he was in charge of new products, he brought up the subject of a gin by Chivas Brothers once again. Not only was the research even more compelling this time around, but he also found a name that made the product clearly *by* Chivas. All he wanted was a real-world test market with an action standard;

if this gin product failed to improve Chivas Regal sales, the idea would be dropped. Reasonable.

While I still didn't have a Ph.D. in OAD, I had a master's and strong survival instincts. I approached the subject gingerly, and discussed it with a family confidante/consultant to gauge the reaction. Instead of debating the merits or concerns, that gentleman must have gone to Edgar Sr. complaining about the idea. (Talk about ass-kissers.)

The next thing I know, I get a poison-pen email from the chairman, the content of which I will never forget:

"If I ever hear the words Chivas and gin used again in the same sentence, heads will roll, starting with yours."

This missive came from the same office that had pushed such brilliant new product ideas as Von Konig Silberwasser (I think it was supposed to be a vodka), Bourbon Street Bourbon (billed as a New Orleans-style bourbon, whatever that is), and my personal favorite, Chivas Danu, whose relationship to scotch continues to elude me. (More to come on this).

Despite the amused reaction from my management, who assured me not to be concerned, the dispatch rankled me, and I avoided both new products and Sam for some time afterward.

Seagram, Bronfman and Chivas Regal

After the aforementioned debacle, the search for updating and strengthening Chivas Regal continued...

"Edgar M. Bronfman, Who Brought Elegance and Expansion to Seagram, Dies at 84" is the headline from the *New York Times* obituary.

I didn't know Edgar Sr. (or the Chairman, as he was known) very well, but interacted with him on many occasions, mainly when Edgar Jr. was off doing his Hollywood thing.

On one occasion, when I was running U.S. marketing, I was summoned (along with my new products guru, Sam Ellias) to Edgar Sr.'s office to tell us about a new product idea for Chivas Regal. Apparently, while on a trip to Europe to survey the state of the business there, a young brand manager suggested to him that Chivas needed to be more contemporary, and she had just the idea for how to do it—a line extension with a more intriguing and youthful brand proposition.

Chivas Regal had been losing market share for years, and any ideas to drastically change the brand's fortune were usually rejected somewhere along the line, as you just read. That the Chairman should be willing to embrace a new scotch brand under the Chivas banner was very welcome news.

The brand manager in Europe suggested that we introduce a product called Chivas De Danu, named for a Celtic goddess who spent eternity with her youthful followers living a life somewhere between bacchanalia and debauchery. (Not exactly right, but close.) I suppose the idea was that if you drank Chivas De Danu, you would stay young forever and always get laid.

The problem was, although the Chairman referred to it correctly when I was first summoned to his office, he later kept referring to it as Chivas Duna, pronounced as in Charlie the *Tuna*. Sam and I were perplexed, and looked it up online (this was the late 1990s and even then, the world was at our fingertips). Sure enough, it was Danu (as in Danube) not Duna.

Now, the hard part. We needed to tell him that while he got it right originally, a product named Chivas de Duna was not going anywhere in the market, after the laughter stopped. The product needed to be called Chivas De *Danu*.

Sam and I nervously set up a meeting with Edgar Sr. Surprisingly, neither of us got our heads chopped off, and he listened attentively to our information—but remained a bit skeptical. He had a brand new computer in his office, and was in the process of learning how to use it, so he challenged us by rushing to his computer to look it up.

He attempted to turn it on, but nothing happened. He grew frustrated and angry and yelled for his assistant, Maxine, to "get that asshole from IT—or whatever they're called—here immediately."

Within moments (most of us waited days for help), someone appeared and sheepishly asked what was the matter. I recall the IT person had a look on his face akin to a prisoner going to the gallows, and his knees were shaking so much, he could hardly stand. Before the Chairman could turn his anger on the poor guy, Maxine interrupted and told Edgar he had a call. With a wave of his hand as he walked off, he indicated that we should work with the IT person to fix the problem and learn the answer.

The two of us hovered over the poor IT fellow as he tried to fix the Chairman's computer. It took one second. He leaned over and tugged on the electric cord and showed us the computer wasn't plugged in. "I thought so," he said, "that's what the problem was last week when I went to his home to fix the computer there."

Computer fixed, information retrieved, and there was the irrefutable evidence that the brand should be called Chivas De Danu. When Edgar returned and saw it for himself, there was a shrug. None of us had the courage to tell him what was wrong with his computer.

By the way, the brand failed miserably.

Roughing it — A Vodka Fable

The chairman of a global spirits company decided that he wanted to build a distillery in the land of his ancestors in Eastern Europe. After all, he reasoned, the communist regimes had recently fallen, and since most countries in the region were impoverished, it would be economically beneficial for all. The country was known for its vodka capabilities (not to mention consumption), and had the manufacturing infrastructure. With some upgrading and reasonable investment, world-class vodka could be produced and sold by his company, which desperately needed imported vodka.

Perhaps the rudiments of manufacturing infrastructure existed, but everything else in the country was in a state of economic disrepair.

Nevertheless, the wheels were set in motion. The executive in charge of the European business unit was given the assignment of making it happen.

Things moved along well. A plant with capacity for expanded growth was found, production experts were engaged, top-notch grain was somehow located, distillation and formulae were worked out, and the plant began to produce vodka.

Proud of the achievement his idea set into motion, the chairman decided that he would come to officially open the factory and visit with the leaders of the newly democratized country. He also thought it would be a good idea to meet with the leaders at a lakefront villa or *dacha*.

This was a major problem for the executive in charge. Even the most lavish dachas were shabby and dilapidated, and the chairman and his entourage were used to the very best.

What to do? His colleagues in New York told him to spare no expense. The chairman was known for his anger, and disappointing him would be a career ender.

So the head of Europe found a dacha, engaged workmen from the country, and flew in top-notch carpenters and plumbers from England to assist. Floors and ceilings were repaired, electricity was enhanced, plastering and painting took place, and the run-down dacha was transformed. Furnishings were rented and flown in.

About a week before the scheduled arrival, the team realized that getting food the chairman would enjoy was an additional problem. No worries: a container of provisions was purchased in London and flown in.

All was set for the arrival of the chairman, after much last-minute scurrying and concerted effort.

His private plane was met, and since it was late at night, the entourage was driven right to the dacha, and they all went to bed.

The next morning, the executive arrived at the dacha and was asked by the chairman to join him at breakfast, which was an elaborate meal.

The executive (holding his breath) said, "So, Chairman, how did you enjoy your first night?"

To which the chairman replied, "Oh you know me, I'm used to roughing it in these third world countries."

"OH YOU KNOW ME, I'M USED TO ROUGHING IT IN THESE THIRD WORLD COUNTRIES."

The Bronfmans

If you talk to former Seagram employees about the Bronfmans, you'll get a wide range of reactions. Edgar M. Bronfman's contributions to the wealth and well-being of the family business are undeniable. Certainly his philanthropic efforts, particularly his stewardship of the World Jewish Congress, reveals a person who understood the need to give back. Yet there are former employees who will tell you that he was quick to anger and to strike out because of both the serious and insignificant actions of employees. He was regal in bearing and not a man to mess with, whether he paid your salary or not.

I recall many instances at hotels, restaurants, or events where someone from Seagram paved the way for Edgar Sr., making sure his needs and wants were catered to. There were many stories, real or imagined, about his temper and the results of disappointing him. The one that sticks out (probably a Seagram myth) was about the poor executive who met the company plane with a white limousine rather than a black one. It was the only one he could get on short notice, and it cost him his job.

So if you could, you avoided the Chairman. In fact, the late Jerry Mann (more about him later) once told me that he had a Ph.D. in Bronfman Avoidance.

The better course of action was to anticipate his needs and take preemptive steps to keep him happy; which I always thought was the most important job of a salesperson in New York City. Selling Seagram products was secondary to making sure the company's brands were available at the restaurant or bar he went to.

On one occasion, his office called to inform a metro NY manager that one of the Chairman's favorite after-theater nightcap spots did not carry Martell Cordon Bleu, and would he make sure that they stocked it. So off he went to the restaurant, and tried to convince the owner to take in the product. The owner said, "No, I have enough Cognacs, and besides, I don't like Martell." The salesman was in a bind; he was instructed to get it placed, and would suffer the consequences the next time the Chairman came in—which his espionage revealed would be that night. He told the owner, "You don't understand. The Chairman of Seagram likes to come here after theater, and he wants Martell." "I don't care," said the owner. In desperation, the salesman said, "Look, here are two bottles—consider them samples. They're for you." Despite the fact that at the time Martell Cordon Bleu was retailing for $100 per bottle, and easily $40+ per glass, the owner not only was intransigent, but also became angry. He refused to stock Martell and really didn't care that the Chairman of Seagram would be disappointed. I admired him for that.

The salesman's only recourse was to come clean in advance and "sell" the Chairman's office on a new and better alternative watering hole.

Edgar Bronfman Jr. was different. I often describe his demeanor as "iron fist in velvet glove." Much more patient than his father—but you still didn't want to piss him off. Mistakes were not met with an automatic guillotine. He believed that the only unacceptable mistakes were those made more than once. I rather liked him, and thought that despite the lucky sperm club status, he was smart and knew what he was doing.

Events proved me wrong.

If you speak with other Seagram alums, the best you'll get about Junior is befuddlement with regard to the selling—and ultimately the destruction— of the empire his grandfather built. Seagram was dissolved for $8 billion in 2000, and less than ten years later, Absolut alone was sold for more than double that amount.

*   *   *

The Darker Side of Wealth

An article from the *New York Observer* (Aug 10, 2010):

> *Inherited millions are often fraught with an array of pathologies and dysfunctions. In 1987, Joanie Bronfman, then a Brandeis philosophy doctoral candidate and the daughter of Edgar Bronfman Sr.'s cousin Gerald, investigated the peculiar psychoses of the rich in her dissertation The Experience of Inherited Wealth: A Social-Psychological Perspective. In the course of her research, she attended "wealth conferences" and interviewed heirs and heiresses. Drawing from her own experience of growing up "visibly wealthy" and full of "shame" as a result of it, Ms. Bronfman argued that inheritors of massive wealth tend to be emotionally stunted. They adopt paranoid worldviews and come to see humans as radically selfish. They perceive relationships to be transactional.*

Their misanthropy derives from the attempts of absentee parents to buy their affections as compensation for outsourcing their rearing to hired professionals. These feelings are reinforced when they interact with the world outside their class and are alternately solicited for donations or mocked as dilettantes by the media. It was that last many-tentacled villain she accused of promulgating a destructive bias toward inheritors, one that she termed "wealthism."

Maybe it should be called the unlucky sperm club.

*   *   *

The Employees – The Toilers in the Vineyard

One of my favorite Seagram employee expressions that partly captured what it was like to work there was, "You'll never become a millionaire working at Seagram, but you'll sure live like one."

The events we ran were world-class and special, and while they may have appeared to be boondoggles, all were important business events that captured the hearts and minds of distributors. A well-known event was the Seagram Family Association (SFA), referred to earlier, which began as a learning tool for the new generation of distributors in the 1950s. Over the years, the learning evolved and kept management and distributors up to date on important business issues, ranging from inventory control to customer relationship management. But make no mistake, these events were held at the foremost hotels and resorts in the U.S. Other events, like the Seagram Achievement Awards (national or regional), came with unbounded geographic restrictions like, Paris, Hong Kong, and international cruises.

The other popular Seagram employee expression was, "The best revenge is a good meal." We might have had our butts kicked at brand and quarterly review meetings during the day, but the dinners were spectacular.

Here are some stories about the toilers in the vineyards.

*   *   *

Those Seagram Folks

I was talking to a fellow Seagram alum, and the conversation turned to what made Seagram unique and where past employees are today.

He pointed out that ex-Seagram people occupy top positions in many companies in the industry. (As of this posting and book.)

He's right; all of the top spirits companies have former Seagram people in very senior spots. When you think about it further, the Seagram folks play important roles throughout the industry: suppliers, distributors, retailers, and service providers.

I suppose it's because of what characterized the company, back in the day. Seagram people learned to adapt, survive, flourish, and succeed because of the common enemy; sort of like a successful person who grew up with dysfunctional parents, but knew he could survive if he relied on his siblings. In short, it's called camaraderie.

They did us a favor by shutting the lights.

The Best Meal in Town

To a large extent, the Booze Business is in the entertainment industry, with food and drink at the core. After a hard day of meetings, conflicts, and difficult decisions, people in the industry go to dinner—partly for business, partly to get to know the local colleagues/adversaries, and partly for the meal.

One of the senior Seagram executives was known for his love of Italian food. He was and is a real gourmet, with knowledge of pasta, sauces, and the differences among regional Italian cuisines.

One day he found himself in Montgomery, Alabama on a market visit. It was a long day of meetings with the trade, consumers, and local Seagram people.

At the end of the day, the Seagram manager said in a southern drawl, "Well boss, it's been a long, hard day and I know how you enjoy your eye-talian food, and ah've arranged for us to have dinnah at the best eye-talian restaurant in Montgomery."

"Really?" said the worn-out exec. "Where are we going?"

"The best place in town...Olive Garden."

Charity

A number of years ago, I read that the Wine & Spirits Division Dinner of the UJA-Federation of NY was honoring a long-time industry executive whose family has been in the business for generations. It reminded me of my experience with United Jewish Appeal (UJA) dinners.

I came to Seagram as the VP Marketing Research, so I started in a senior position. That was in the spring of 1986. Three months later, I received a memo telling me to report to The Glenlivet Tavern on the 5th floor of 375 Park Ave for the UJA "meeting" of the executive group. I had no idea what to make of this gathering. The people who were on my staff said things like "Uh oh, they are going to call you by name and expect you to announce your contribution to the annual spirits and wine fund drive for the UJA; going to cost you lots of money, but don't worry, the company will match your gift." What?

I quickly realized that 1) This was organized extortion 2) I didn't want to appear stingy 3) I also didn't want to appear obsequious, and 4) It was a good cause, but why did I have to stand up and publically declare my gift? I later learned it was the "tithe" that made the family look good. Although in fairness, I should add that the Bronfmans always made a significant contribution in their own right. But their gift, plus the executives' gift, plus matching funds, meant that the Seagram "family" would be giving enough to sustain a small developing nation for a year.

I came to the decision that I had to do what I had to do, and decided on a number that my staff had suggested. You don't want to know how much. It was over the top.

So I was locked and loaded and ready for the "calling of names" at the meeting. Unbeknownst to me, the other executives had been through this many times before, and knew how to beat the system. They called each other beforehand and decided on the amount that would be given by each managerial level. (Hey friends, thanks for telling me!)

Since my name begins with an S, I had ample opportunity to see what my associates were giving. My planned contribution was way out of whack. I quickly made a readjustment downward.

Lesson learned: After only 3 months, I realized it was "us against them."

I also learned that the advice you got from some people was not necessarily reliable. In short, I got the lay of the land pretty quickly.

Please forgive me if the UJA is not at the top of my charitable giving list.

Blame the Bronfmans.

Takeout Food Seagram-style

Like many companies in the food, beverage, and hospitality industry, Seagram cocktail receptions and meals were somewhere between elaborate and over the top. A long list of starving countries could feed their people from the leftovers of a cocktail reception.

Two stories come to mind.

Just before the sale of the company, a world-class global marketing person was hired to unify the disparate marketing and communications efforts around the world. He was a pretty decent guy with a long pedigree and great skills at managing upward. Above all, he was a top-notch eater. At company-related events involving food, he always seemed to have a look on his face akin to orgasmic pleasure.

I wasn't there at the time, but at least a dozen marketing people told the story of a particular eating incident in London. The cocktail reception for customers was the usual elaborate affair, with passed hors d'oeuvres and a buffet designed with both the gourmet and gourmand in mind. As the evening progressed, the new head of marketing's entourage reminded the gentleman in question that they needed to move on to a business dinner. He was reluctant to leave; particularly as the grilled lamb chops were being offered. They pressed him, and he grudgingly agreed to go, but not before he grabbed three or four of the succulent gems from the tray.

The team was astonished. They reminded him that there was no time to eat them, since the car was waiting. Undeterred, he proceeded to stuff the lamb chops into each of his front jacket pockets and head for the car.

In the car, on the way to the business dinner, he happily chomped away at his prize, as his colleagues stared at each other in total dismay.

I was there when the other story took place.

It was at a meeting in Canada at a Four Seasons hotel. We had been very busy touring the market and learning about the Canadian spirits industry. The plan was to meet in the lobby, then head off for dinner with our Canadian hosts.

Adjacent to the lobby was a bar with a tray of delectable nibbles, including sushi. One of my colleagues, also known for his voracious appetite, spotted the tray, assumed they were munchies for the guests, and before anyone could say a word, grabbed some sushi. Obviously, he was famished. After all, it must have been two or three hours since we last ate.

Just as he was about to pop the sushi in his mouth, we heard a shriek, and the beverage manager ran up to him shouting, "Don't eat that...it's a display, and the food has been there all afternoon."

Sheepishly, he tossed the errant sushi in the trash. But for a moment, he looked like he didn't believe her, and debated eating it anyhow. Twenty minutes is a long time to wait for dinner when you're hungry.

"I'LL SAVE THESE FOR LATER."

Keeper of the "goodies"

Like many companies that entertain customers and clients, Seagram had a designated employee who handled customer/trade events and trips, national sales incentive programs, and—the big prize—season tickets to sporting events in the NYC area.

One of these individuals, who I will call Mr. Keeper, was a nice and friendly guy until the subject of tickets came up. He didn't see himself merely as the guardian or custodian of the coveted seats. Oh no—he was the protector, the *de facto* owner. Requests for tickets to a game were more often than not subjected to interrogation, as to the identity of the intended customer and the rationale behind the request. And invariably, unless the requestor was of significant "rank," the request was denied outright or it so happened that "someone else already got them."

The management of the U.S. operation passed to a new team, and Mr. Keeper got an assignment outside of the U.S. operation, but still based in NYC.

The team that took over had its own designated employee to handle the customer relations, events, and incentive trips. But when the first need for ballgame tickets arose, Mr. Keeper informed the new designate that the seats would be staying with Mr. Keeper, and doled out as he saw fit.

Needless to say, the new team was incensed, and a (gentle) management skirmish erupted. But with bigger issues to be addressed, the matter was set aside—if not forgotten.

One day, a senior executive asked for and grudgingly received tickets to an important Mets game. While he knew the general vicinity on the field level where the seats were located, he wasn't sure as to the exact location. He stopped an usher at the top of the section and handed the tickets to him. The usher looked at the tickets, looked at the executive, then back at the tickets, then at the executive again.

"Anything wrong?" asked the executive.

"Oh no," said the usher. "I'm just surprised that you're sitting in Mr. Keeper's seats."

For all I know, he still has those seats.

Business in the Bush

There were two couples and a pilot on the small plane as it returned from sightseeing in the African countryside. They were heading for the "base camp" some 20 minutes away. Actually, base camp was a misnomer; it should have been referred to as the Ritz in the Jungle.

It was a very elaborate sales incentive trip that a spirits company decided to offer its distributors, in order to outdo Seagram. From what I'm told, this was indeed a spectacular trip.

No one really knows what caused the eruption and noise coming from one of the distributors' stomachs. It could have been the huge breakfast, maybe the elaborate dinner the night before, perhaps jetlag, or even the water. Possibly, it was all of the above.

Whatever the cause, the big guy in the back row was in distress. "Hey pilot, I got some stomach trouble...real bad...how long 'til we land?"

The pilot's answer was far from comforting. "About 20 minutes. Can't go much faster."

"You don't understand son, I can't last that long. Isn't there any place closer where you can land?" howled the distributor.

"Not really," said the pilot.

By now, the other three people in the plane were also in distress, worrying about his discomfort and the elevated sounds coming from the distributor. "Please," said his wife, "isn't there anything you can do?"

"Well...Okay, I have an idea," the pilot offered. "There is a flat area without brush just ahead. I think I can land...it'll be a bit choppy...not too bad...just hang on."

Sure enough, the pilot landed with a few bumps, but it was a surprisingly smooth touchdown for the middle of the jungle.

"Now what?" asked the distributor.

"As soon as I stop, leave the plane and head about 200 yards to that brush area, and do what you got to do."

The plane had barely come to a stop when he jumped out and did a combination crab-walk and jog for the foliage.

A few minutes later, he walked out of the brush with a smile on his face. Ran to the plane, got in, and the pilot immediately took off.

Somewhere in eastern Africa, there is a bushman who tells the villagers the story of how he was tending his flock, and out of nowhere, an airplane lands. A big white man jumps out of the plane into the bush, makes awful body noises, jumps back into the plane, and off they go.

To this day the bushman must be telling his friends he has no idea about how or why this happened. But it was surely the strangest thing he had ever seen. It took hours to round up his flock.

If it were a Seagram trip, there would have been a bathroom on the plane.

Limousines

Nearly all the business executives I know who use car services for travel avoid limousines in favor of sedans. One exception is when there is a large group, so a limousine is more cost-effective. The other is the old-school type of executive (now few and far between), who think they are impressing suppliers by picking them up in a long, black vehicle.

However, the car service companies sometimes feel they are rewarding a good client by "upgrading" them to a limousine from a town car.

I remember an occasion at the end of a long trip that culminated in an offsite meeting in the New York area, and the concern I felt when I was told, "Since you are such a good customer, we are sending a limo." "Please don't; it's not necessary." The reply: "It's on us, no extra charge."

"You don't understand," I said. "My associates will be picked up in sedans or drive their own cars, and there is no way I want them to think that I use limos ... which I don't."

"I'm sorry," the dispatcher said, "but the car is on the way and should be there in 10 minutes."

In a near panic, I replied, "Listen, call him and tell him to stay at the entrance and I'll come down the hill to him. No way I want to be picked up at the main entrance."

So my luggage and I walked half a mile, and like someone who was on the run or had something to hide, I looked left and right a dozen times before I got in the limo. If I could have disguised myself, I would have. I got away undetected.

Someone else I knew was not so lucky.

The company plane came back from a trip. It could have been the retreat at Ivy Creek or a Tunnel of Love tour (see next story) to the regions. I can't remember which. It was raining; no, make that pouring. The plane— Whiskey 7—pulled up to the hanger at Westchester Airport and stopped. The tarmac was full of car service vehicles waiting to pick us up.

When the crew opened the door and dropped the stairs, a driver from the limousine at the head of the line ran up the stairs with an umbrella. We all thought it was for Edgar Jr. But in a loud voice he declared, "Mr. A, please?"

Out of the back of the plane, more than a bit sheepish, Mr. A said, (in a very low voice) "Be right there."

Mr. A was known as someone who did a great job for the company, but also liked his creature comforts.

As he walked down the stairs, and the rest of us waited, Junior said, "See you tomorrow... Stretch."

He was known as Stretch evermore.

To this day, I don't know if he was a victim of an overzealous car company, or a guy who got caught.

Tunnel of Love Tour

I first heard this expression when I was running Seagram America's marketing, and went with the CEO to visit markets in South America.

His view of senior management market visits can be summed up best as follows: "What a waste of time. Everything we will see in the stores will be staged for our visit. It's a tunnel of love tour, but we need to do it."

I felt he kind of missed the point. Market visits were, and still are, designed to "see how we look;" and in that regard, it's in the human condition to put your best foot forward. But you can't stage how the competition looks, and what they are up to at point of sale. And who can control what Mr. Retailer has to say?

My favorite tunnel of love anecdote took place in a large, important U.S. market known more for its on-premise business than retail stores. Nevertheless, the distributor wanted to show us how good he and our local marketing and sales reps were doing, and how our floor programs stood out.

The entourage—a better description might be the sheriff and the posse—went off on the visit/tour, and once inside a store, some spoke to the owner or manager while others checked the displays and floor programs.

A member of the group was fascinated by a multi-case display of one of our brands, and the very large and attractive case card that accompanied it. Never having seen it before, and admiring it, he called others over to have a look. Someone touched the case card and to his surprise, smudged it. It was hand-painted... and still wet. We all smiled at what appeared to be a permanent holiday display that was obviously just put up for our visit. "That's okay," someone said, "maybe it'll stay up. And look how much real estate the brands have."

Smiles turned to laughter at the next stop, also a large store with a massive display right at the entrance.

There was the same case card with the same smudge in the same spot.

I have no idea how they moved that thing so quickly.

*   *   *

The Company Plane

Among the Seagram stories I have not written much about is that of the company plane. Or should I say air fleet, since it consisted of multiple Gulf Stream Jets and a few helicopters.

The use of the company plane was more than a frivolous perk. Firstly, it was an efficient, not to mention cost effective, way for executives to visit 6 to 8 markets in one week. For the executives, it meant no security lines, being met at the private airport by local colleagues with the key to your hotel room, and no hassle whatsoever. Never mind the absence of frequent flyer miles—this was the way to travel.

But sometimes there were unpleasant side effects, most notably, no place to hide when all 14 seats were occupied by an assortment of colleagues and the brass.

On one occasion, we were returning from the signing of the Absolut distribution agreement. Quite a joyous occasion: we had not only filled the very large gap in the portfolio with world-class premium vodka, but the victory was sweet, since we had beaten our competition. The company plane was full of execs, including Edgar Jr. I was sitting with a group at a table when Junior came over and said, "Arturo," (oh, how I loathed that nickname) "I have some advice on the marketing of Absolut." There was silence, except for the clicking of pens in order to scribe the words of wisdom about to be uttered. All he had to say was, "Don't fuck it up." (See the Chapter 8 about vodka for the full story.)

* * *

Where to sit?

The protocol on where to sit on the company plane was well known. The owner, either Edgar Sr. or Edgar Jr., had the last seat on the right as you faced the rear of the plane (aft). If they weren't on it, the most senior executive had that seat. Other plush seats were taken by rank, and the couches (we're talking Gulfstream jets), were left to the more junior or lower ranking execs.

As the story goes, while waiting for one of the Bronfmans to board the plane, a company president was talking to a colleague, when suddenly Bronfman appeared. Startled, the executive shot up, moved away, and said, "Sorry Mr. Bronfman, here's your seat." To which the Bronfman in question replied, "They're all my seats."

* * *

A Mann For All Seasons

No book about Seagram and the alcohol industry could be complete without a story or two about the (in)famous Jerry Mann.

I met Jerry when I first came to the company, after most of his exploits had been well underway. Jerry and his sidekick were quite a dynamic duo, the Frick and Frack of the **Booze Business**. I sensed that their antics, with Jerry as the leader, amused the owners—who while striving for respectability nevertheless admired the Damon Runyon side of the business. However, over time Jerry self-destructed, while his sidekick continued to be in favor and was ultimately well-rewarded by the family.

The first time I met Jerry Mann, he was president of one of the Seagram companies. It was during my initial round of interviews. We got along, and I recall how impressed I was with him. In all my previous years as a consultant, having met scores of "captains of industry," none were as charming as Jerry. In fact, at the end of the interview, he did the most extraordinary thing: he gave me his business card, wrote his home number on it, and said something like, "Listen pal, if you have any questions or want to know anything more about the company, call me." We both knew that it was a gesture; he was not going to be the one to hire me, and there was no way I would call him. Nevertheless, I was impressed.

Over the years and after Seagram, I learned that not everyone who knew him thought as much of him as I did. To me, Jerry was a larger-than-life character who smoked and drank too much, gambled too much, and—well—couldn't keep his dick in his pants.

Here was this short, slightly overweight, not particularly handsome man with a stable of women ready to throw themselves into his bed. I say this with wonder, not envy. All I can surmise is that his charm, character, and power as a top executive was an aphrodisiac for many women.

My first such encounter was at a sales meeting in Las Vegas; he asked me to join him at his front row table. As the chorus of beauties pranced around the stage, he leaned over and asked me which one I wanted. I laughed, thinking he was kidding. He wasn't. I just looked at him and said, "No thanks."

My last encounter with Jerry was a few days after I took over as head of U.S. marketing. My first order of business was to downsize (remember that term?) the marketing department. Such was the state of business affairs in those days, particularly at Seagram. The 60s and 70s were full of employee growth, mostly unnecessary, and the 80s and 90s were payback.

In any event, one of the victims of my required staff reduction was a known friend of Jerry's... a very *good* friend, if you catch my drift. At this time, the Seagram game of musical executive chairs had landed Jerry in a benign "kicked upstairs" position. His glory days had come to a close. Nevertheless, I felt I owed it to him to give a heads up that his friend was going to be let go. So early the next morning, I went to his office to tell him the news.

When I walked in, he said, "Hey pal, I heard the good news, congrats." "Thanks, Jerry," I said, "But there's something I need to tell you." His puffing on the ever-present cigarette intensified. "Oh yeah?" Somehow I think he knew what was coming. I explained that part of my ticket of admission to head of marketing was cost control and downsizing. I went on in an almost apologetic tone to inform him that his "friend" would be a victim. He lit another cigarette, paused, looked at me closely and said, "Too bad, pal. Just this morning, under this desk, she gave me the best...." I interrupted him, turned bright red, told him I didn't want to know, stammered something about "she'll be taken care of by HR," and left the room.

That was my last encounter with one of the most colorful characters I've ever known. I think that episode marked the beginning of the downfall, as the demons finally got hold of him.

*   *   *

Bronfman Royalty

On the trip I described a few pages ago, all the brass was in attendance at the Absolut signing in Stockholm. At the lower end of the totem pole were the staff people— the finance guy and myself. So while the grownups adjourned to iron out the last minute details, our Swedish counterparts escorted him and I on a tour of the city.

Among the sites we visited was the Vasa Museum, which housed the warship Vasa. The ship sank on her maiden voyage from Stockholm in 1628, and was salvaged in 1961. It's the only preserved 17th century ship in the world.

That night, when we all convened for celebratory cocktails and dinner, Edgar Jr. asked what we had seen and done on the tour that day. I told him about the Vasa, and how amazing the restoration had been. I went on to say, "The King of Sweden at the time wanted a battle ship like no other during a war with Poland. He commissioned this ship, and insisted it have twice the number of cannons than any other ship at the time. It was so heavy and unstable that it sank almost immediately in the harbor, about 1,400 yards from where it was launched." I went on, "Can you imagine a king insisting on such folly?" or words to that effect.

Edgar Jr. looked at me coldly and said, "I'm sure it was because of his advisors."

To this day, I'm not sure whether he was kidding or sending a message.

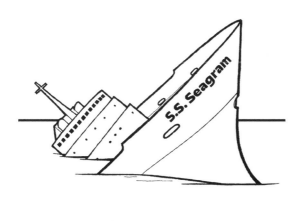

*   *   *

How the Toilers Almost Became the Owners

The last chapter in this book describes the events surrounding the closing of the Seagram Spirits and Wine Company. But a brief story might be in order here.

Between the time when it was announced that the company would be sold and split up between two rival companies (ultimately, Diageo and Pernod Ricard), and the closing of the deal, it was not widely known that there was another option: the employees.

Most of the senior executives were prepared to use their resources (stock options, 401k money, personal savings, etc.) to buy the company via an employee ownership program. Together with some investors, the family was approached with a plan that might have been better than all offers—or so I was led to believe.

While I wasn't privy to the discussions, the prevalent rumor was that the offer was angrily, and incredulously (as in, "how dare you?") brushed aside.

It was a pity; not only would the family and shareholders do well, but the legacy of the Seagram company, and all that Mr. Sam had built, would remain intact.

I never heard a good explanation—but I, for one, believe it was a childish move based on "if I don't want it, then you can't have it" and/or "oh my... what if they succeed?"

3. Brand Stories—It's all in how you tell it

One of my favorite marketing gurus, who I follow closely, is Seth Godin. Here is one of the more interesting definitions he has about a brand and branding:

A brand is the set of expectations, memories, stories and relationships that, taken together, account for a consumer's decision to choose one product or service over another. If the consumer (whether it's a business, a buyer, a voter or a donor) doesn't pay a premium, make a selection or spread the word, then no brand value exists for that consumer.

In the last chapter, I wrote about Jerry Mann, and while he was far from a marketing expert, he had an interesting way of describing brands, imagery, and people.

Jerry drank only Seagram's Gin, a basic, no frills product with a very strong black consumer following, dating back to the end of prohibition. To Jerry, Seagram's was the Real McCoy, and he drank it straight, on the rocks. I once told him that we needed to grow the brand beyond the current market, or purchase a top shelf brand. He disagreed. "The average white male gin drinker is a fraud. When he's in a bar and wants to impress a woman or his friends, he orders Beefeater; at home, he drinks Seagram's."

He didn't use marketing speak, but instinctively understood the consumer of spirits. What was considered "fraud" to Jerry Mann is called "making an impression." But he also understood that in few other businesses could a person create an impression, an image of themselves, by only paying a few extra dollars for a name brand drink. I may be struggling to make ends meet; but for an extra $5, I can have a top shelf brand at a bar, and prove to the world and myself that I have made it.

*   *   *

Brand Icons

There are a number of definitions of what makes a brand an icon; including immediate recognition, longevity, distinctiveness in the market place, and having a deep connection with consumers.

There are a few current icon brands in the spirits market, but there are many more "used to be," than still are. Among the bygone icons, I think Absolut heads the list. The brand had an exalted status in the 1980s and 90s. When Seagram closed, the Swedes decided to be masters of their own fate, launched a U.S. company, and went at it on their own. Unfortunately, the ex-Seagram executive they put in charge totally blew it, and the brand began its decline. By the time they woke up and hired an excellent CEO (also a Seagram alum), it was too late. Once a brand slips, it's extraordinarily difficult to bring it back to exalted status. Just like Humpty Dumpty.

Another fallen icon is Grey Goose. Under the watchful eye of Sidney Frank, the brand rose to the top, on the basis of what I call the outrageous factor. This consisted of: a unique, see-through bottle; a peculiar and memorable name; a vodka from France; and above all, a $35 price point, when all other top shelf vodkas (including Absolut, at the time) were selling for half the price. Taken together, these factors made a statement, and the brand stood out. But its iconic image and status began to erode when Bacardi bought it. With all due respect to Bacardi, a brand built by an entrepreneur often encounters problems in a corporate structure.

Patron Tequila and Johnnie Walker are just a few of the brands that have maintained their iconic status over the years. You may have others in mind—like Jack Daniel's, Crown Royal, or Captain Morgan. The list of pretenders to the throne is long. But let's not confuse popularity with iconic status.

In this chapter, we will meet all sorts of brands, and try to dissect their success or lack thereof.

Let's start with my favorite: Captain Morgan, a used-to-be iconic brand.

*   *   *

The Captain Morgan Story

How a Seagram orphan brand became an icon.

Despite the problems the brand has encountered in recent years, Captain Morgan Original Spiced Rum changed the spirits industry in a number of ways. It was the first brand that managed to put a dent in the rum category powerhouse, by the strategic use of flavoring. Furthermore, the brand pioneered the important role of flavors, a phenomenon we take for granted today.

In the early 1980s, the new products group at Seagram was charged with filling gaps in the company's portfolio. At the time, spirits sales were languishing and unlike more recent times, whiskies were on the decline. So the gaps that needed to be filled were in the so-called white goods arena, with rum at the top of the list. The brands already in the stable were either price-driven (Ron Rico), or weak and on life support (Palo Viejo). Myers's rum, the upmarket brand, was (and still is) a small volume brand, limited to specialty drink usage. In addition, the product is outside the traditional white, light rum taste profile.

The new products group engaged Kahn Associates, headed by Bernie Kahn, a former creative director at Grey Advertising. Mr. Kahn's claim to fame was the slogan "Choosy Moms Choose Jif," which propelled the brand to number one in peanut butter.

The key issue behind the assignment: How do you go up against an 800-pound gorilla like Bacardi, which controls an overwhelming share of the rum category?

Consequently, it was clear to everyone that the only viable pathway was a "value added" proposition. Unless you have a boatload of money to go head to head with a dominant market leader, go for an indirect approach and outflank them. Even with a ton of marketing funding, taking on Bacardi was more than likely a losing proposition.

Based on the views of the new products people, insights from marketing research, and the advice of Kahn Associates, it was decided that the new rum entry would be a flavored product.

But what flavor, and what to call it?

While there is some ambivalence about how the decision to go with spice came about, it was clear that two hurdles needed to be overcome. First, since the vast majority of rum drinks are mixed (and at the time, predominantly with cola), the flavor had to accommodate a mixed drink such as rum and coke. Second, flavoring and tastes can be polarizing (love it or hate it), so the flavor to be chosen had to have wide appeal.

The decision was reached to add vanilla and call it "Spiced Rum." Vanilla and the other ingredients delivered a pleasant, desirable taste, and the vague word "spiced" added mystery and avoided automatic rejection. Not only that, but the word "spiced" allowed consumers to project what they thought it might taste like, and the flavorings lived up to the promise. A winning formula was born.

But what about branding?

Here is where Seagram's corporate culture entered the picture. Everyone had an opinion, and thought everyone else's opinion stank (to paraphrase an old, off-color expression). So the brand name fell into one of those vicious corporate cycles, wherein a proposal goes round and round and no decision emerges. To compound matters, names that had broad management support turned out to be already trademarked and unavailable.

At last, someone realized that the company owned a brand in the U.K. called Captain Morgan. A star was born.

Now the problem was which company to place it in.

At the time, Seagram had four operating divisions handling the spirits business. They consisted of Seagram (Seagram-named brands), General Wine and Spirits (the upmarket brands), Calvert (price and push brands) and Summit (the brand hospice). Both the Seagram and General Wine and Spirits divisions were out, because they already had rums, and there is no way a newborn brand could go to Summit.

That left Calvert Distillers, the home of Calvert Gin and Lord Calvert

Canadian, among others. (People at Seagram used to joke that Lord Calvert Canadian's popularity was its square bottle. That meant it wouldn't roll out of the back of the truck.)

In retrospect, putting Captain Morgan into Calvert was a gutsy decision. After all, the Calvert marketing and sales people were used to pushing their brands with little consumer pull, and relied on pricing and point of sale promotions to move the goods. In fact, the people who worked at Calvert were looked down upon by others at the Seagram Corporation, and were paid less than their counterparts at the other divisions.

Maybe putting the new brand into Calvert was a magnanimous gesture on the part of management, or maybe it was a plot to kill the brand, or even a cruel joke. But I think that the single most important factor in the success of the brand, while at Seagram, was due to the Calvert people.

Picture this. You're a sales person at the Calvert Distillers Division of Seagram; and to put it bluntly, you're viewed as the runt of the litter, always sucking hind tit. The brands you're selling are a challenge, and you're making less money than your counterpart two floors above you in the same Seagram building. To quote Rodney Dangerfield, "You don't get no respect."

Suddenly, a new rum product falls in your lap. The product tastes great, there's a story behind it, and above all, it's a fun brand whose allure is not based on pricing and discounting. There is the potential for great drink night promotions at bars (the Captain and the Morganettes), and outstanding retail point-of-sale items.

The Calvert people go to work with strong motivation, zest and zeal, and something to prove to their colleagues in other divisions. Their sales philosophy departed from the usual, and instead of loading up retailers, all initial orders were limited, thereby encouraging reorders. Aggressively, they went after sampling opportunities with drink nights and co-packing small sizes with Coke.

The rest is history. The test marketing (1982) was a huge success, and by 1983 the brand went national.

By the early 1990s (under my watch), while the brand was a winner, there were some hurdles in the way of further growth. Captain Morgan was amber rum, and the preponderance of consumption was light/clear.

Furthermore, Malibu had come on the scene with a coconut flavor. Above all, Bacardi gave up waiting for Captain Morgan to fail, woke up, and came after us by introducing their version of spiced rum. Their proposition was that that the Captain was for younger drinkers, and their product was intended for the mature and serious rum aficionado.

Our response was line and brand extensions, with specific strategic roles. Each of the three extensions had an objective, going beyond shelf space acquisition and copycat products. A silver version was introduced, and replaced Captain Morgan Coconut, which was a feeble previous attempt to take on Malibu. Instead, that coconut product became Parrot Bay by Captain Morgan, with its own imagery. Finally, Captain Morgan Private Stock was the upmarket entry designed to deal directly with the new Bacardi product.

The overall Captain Morgan franchise, now owned by Diageo, is doing poorly (as of this writing). Their efforts seem to be all over the place, with a range of line extensions that frankly, make little sense. Meanwhile, the base brand languishes.

From what I've seen, the Captain Morgan Original rate of growth over the past five years has been flat. Furthermore, the overall growth for the line has been a function of line extensions at the expense of Original Spiced. (According to a July 2015 story in *Shanken News Daily*, Captain Morgan's sales declined 1.5% from the previous year.)

In fairness to Diageo, the marketplace has changed appreciably. There are a number of spiced rum brands and a few new powerhouse players, including Sailor Jerry and Kraken. Both of these brands have strong taste profiles, and provide a positive image in tune with today's drinker.

Yet if you go to the Captain Morgan web page, you'll find peculiar and tactical line extensions, like 100 proof, Black Spiced rum (a blatant Kraken lookalike), Lime Bite, Tattoo Spiced, Long Island Iced Tea, and even plain old White Rum. Most of the line extensions (9 of them) appear to be declining, and even hurting the original product. This violates the cardinal rule of line extensions: a line extension should feed the base brand, not eat it.

Perhaps Diageo should try to hire former Calvert people.

What makes a brand successful?

When I first started working with Absolut in the mid-90s, the Swedes had an interesting expression about the brand. They referred to it as "an overnight success since 1982." Absolut remains an important powerhouse brand, even amidst the churn and turmoil in the vodka market. Along the way, other "overnight" successes have appeared and faded.

So what's the common denominator? What makes a brand break out of the pack either from the starting gate as a new brand entry, or over time?

Let's start with what it's *not* about.

It's not about market/consumer research. Absolut and Bailey's failed in consumer tests. The old IDV Company had a brand called Greensleeves that broke all consumer test records...*have you ever heard of Greensleeves?* As I mentioned earlier, market research is better at describing behavior than predicting it.

And it's not about big marketing and advertising budgets. Even when the mass media dinosaurs ruled the earth, no spirit company could afford to break through the clutter. The advent of the digital communications era may change that, but it will take time and patience.

There's one good success inhibitor: patience. The large spirits companies generally don't have the time or fortitude to nurture new brands or to enhance the growth of burgeoning brands. Throughout the system—from spirits marketers to sales people to wholesalers—the portfolio they handle is cluttered, and the rewards come from the known winners.

The big companies are good at taking new brands and products and moving them to new heights. They don't create brands—they buy them. Once they buy a brand, there's an economic (or career) incentive to show it was a good move. That's when things begin to happen.

But success from the outset depends on vision, tenacity, and the trade.

Let's look at it another way.

In my experience, it's three commercial "buckets" in the following order: the manufacturer, the trade, and the consumer.

Yes, in the **Booze Business**, before you get to market/sell a brand to consumers, you've got to pass through the first two gates.

Corporations/manufacturers "talk the talk" about brand investment and new product development. But unless there is vision at the top, strong senior management support, tolerance for out-of-the-box thinking, and of course, willingness to take risk, nothing will happen.

People on the street can make or break a brand, even more so than consumers. Sure, it's about incentives, but it's also about involvement, managing expectations, and reorders—not just placement.

Consider this: A salesperson sells two cases of a new brand, and the retailer moves 6 bottles in a few weeks. Chances are he/she will see the brand as a slow mover, because there is a case and a half left. If the retailer had bought one case and 6 were left after a few weeks, the retailer thinks the product is "flying off the shelves."

So as far as the consumer is concerned—and by no means am I minimizing their importance—it's about the trade influence, brand uniqueness, and relevance. Line up all three of these pieces, and you can actually hear the crack of the bat.

*　　*　　*

The single most important influencer in brand building is the bartender. How many times have you said or heard someone else say, "What do you recommend?" Or "What's she drinking...I'll have the same."

When it comes to a new brand or product, the Booze Business provides the opportunity to try or "sample" the product at a bar without buying a bottle.

Smart marketers know that the on-premise is often the key to success. That's why companies use brand ambassadors and product promotions at bars.

*　　*　　*

True Fans

Like many other businesses, the market for alcohol follows the old 20/80 rule; twenty percent of your customers account for 80% of your business.

A recent post by Seth Godin is called "The circles (no more strangers)," and deals with the value of a "true fan" vs. "strangers."

He writes:

Let's say a marketer has $10,000 to spend. Is it better to acquire new customers at $2,000 each (advertising is expensive) or spend $10 a customer to absolutely delight and overwhelm 1,000 true fans?

Crown Royal

Crown Royal is an iconic brand, but it has always been a mystery to me.

When I first encountered it as a consumer, it was the brand my grandfather served when company came over. Philadelphia Whiskey was his usual fare, but his Crown Royal was special.

I'm not a historian on the brand, but at the outset it had important equities and just needed a spark. The taste was great, and unlike other whiskies at the time, it had unique packaging inside and out, a back-story about the royal visit to Canada, and a very aspirational look and feel. The spark occurred when oil workers from Canada who were working in the Gulf of Mexico came to Gulf cities on their night off, with pockets full of money, and wanted the best whiskey they knew from home: Crown Royal.

As the story goes, this set off the growth and proliferation of the brand, primarily in the South.

It was marketed in the Seagram days in a classic brand-building manner. "Push" and "pull" efforts worked together successfully, and the brand grew—even while vodka was also growing by leaps and bounds.

The sales and regional marketing component, orchestrated by Jim Reichardt, was top of the game. All the activity was integrated and based on strategy: from the distributor focus, to programming, to "pull" activity at retail. Above all, carefully considered marketing innovations were introduced under Jimmy's watch.

On the national marketing side, programs were developed to maximize the equity—especially the purple Crown Royal bag in which the product was wrapped—and develop relationships with the core consumer. The advertising was that unique combination of creative excellence combined with brand recognition and sell. Not your average garden-variety ad campaign.

Everything on the brand was done for strategic reasons. The sole line extension (at the time) was Crown Royal Special Reserve, whose intent was to protect the brand's flank from above, and make a price-value statement about the base brand. It was not to make a sales number. In fact, many worried about cannibalization of the base brand, which never occurred. At one point, both were growing at double digits.

I've been checking on Crown Royal and how it's doing for the past 6 or 7 years and there have been lots of ups and downs.

I also noticed that there are 5 Crown Royal products in the line. I think my grandfather would have been confused.

*   *   *

Update:

As of July 2015, according to Shaken News Daily, *Crown Royal's annual growth was flat at 0.7%. While the base brand has been growing more robustly, the line extensions are losing ground. However, more recently, some industry friends have told me that Crown Royal Maple and Crown Royal Apple are exceeding expectations. Go figure.*

*   *   *

Market Research and Crown Royal

I mentioned that Crown Royal's strength was centered in the Southern region of Seagram. This was the case for much of the brand's development. Brand manager after brand manager in annual review meetings presented programs to "move beyond the south." Most efforts failed until the late 1990s, and that was largely a result of breaking the voluntary ban on broadcast advertising. (See Chapter 11).

On one occasion, a brand manager presented a plan to do a deep dive into the brand's consumer franchise. He presented a research plan to conduct an Attitude and Use Study (A&U) to the tune of $200,000, as I recall. While it's probably much more expensive today, it was a good deal of money to learn what I felt we already knew or surmised.

"Okay," I said, "On one condition. The research needs to report all the consumer reasons for the strength of the brand in the south, and determine how applicable those strengths are for the rest of the country." Simple enough.

What came back were tons of numbers, printouts, and the preverbal consumer segmentation study. I was told that it was the best segmentation study the research agency had ever seen—perfectly balanced segments, high correlation factors, and beautiful to look at. The only thing missing was the answer to my question.

*　　*　　*

Seagram and Vodka

Until the "acquisition" of Absolut, Seagram was not just a vodka-less company; it was an Ostrich hiding its head in whiskey, pretending not to see the world of booze change.

Sam Bronfman's aversion/reluctance to sell vodka is widely known. Perhaps for him, liquor needed to be aged or brown or have the word "whiskey" on the bottle. Whatever his reasons, the company was never a vodka player. In fact, when I was in market research, one of the older executives told me the story of how Mr. Sam (the founder) reacted to a research project about changing consumer alcohol tastes. It may be apocryphal, but it sure has the ring of truth.

One of the most notable consumer researchers of the 50s and 60s, Alfred Politz, was an early leader in the techniques of polling and opinion analysis. He was commissioned to do a study of changing consumer alcohol tastes and attitudes. The presentation of the findings took place at an executive retreat, and in an unusual display of bonhomie, Mr. Sam suggested they review the results while sitting around the pool.

Page after page of the report pointed to the potential rise of vodka at the expense of whiskies. Politz was said to have been very clear that the evidence overwhelmingly leaned in this direction. It was also clear that Mr. Sam was getting angrier and angrier. Finally he got up from his chaise, grabbed the report out of the researcher's hands, threw it in the pool, muttered some obscenity, and stormed off. Politz was said to have been relieved not to join his report.

So while competitors were developing Smirnoff, Popov, Stolichnaya, and other brands, Seagram was struggling with entries like Wolfschmidt, Nikolai, and Crown Russe.

At long last, someone decided to create a new vodka brand—but unlike most of those on the market at the time, it was to be imported vodka. In fact, it was called Seagram Imported Vodka or SIV, as it was lovingly referred to. Imported all the way from Canada.

Management at the time knew that the "white goods" race was passing Seagram by, and the pressure to succeed was very strong. So much so that when a presentation to a major California chain was set up to expand distribution, the "brass" decided to attend.

Picture this: Edgar Jr., plus the head of marketing, the head of sales, and brand managers all fly off in the company plane to attend this meeting on SIV. They get to L.A. early, with time to kill before the meeting. Since a few of them had never seen the inside of a chain store liquor department, they decide to visit a few stores.

Next thing you know, there are 4 or 5 suits walking the aisles, checking the shelves, and watching consumers make decisions and purchases. They're paying particular attention to the vodka section, and spot a man looking at the brands and seemingly trying to make a decision. A member of the entourage goes up to him, takes a bottle of SIV off the shelf, hands it to the man, and says, "check this one out...it's imported."

The man studies the bottle for a moment or two, looks at the exec, and as he puts it back on the shelf, says, "that's not imported—it's Seagram."

"It will never sell" vs. "You never know"

In a conversation with my friend and former colleague James Espey (who you will read about more in later chapters), the subject of Baileys Irish Cream came up. For those of you who don't know him or of him, suffice it to say that James is a legend in the spirits industry, as a very senior manager who has successfully run companies, categories, and brands. In addition to creating the Keepers of the Quaich (see next chapter) James' innovation history includes the invention of Malibu, significant involvement in Baileys, Chivas Regal 18, Johnnie Walker Blue, and many more.

[Incidentally, not long ago James was awarded the OBE (Order of the British Empire) by Queen Elizabeth for his efforts on behalf of Scotch whisky over the years.]

Anyway, the subject turned to what it takes for a brand to withstand the naysayers (generally, corporate types who are risk adverse and would rather buy a proven brand than create one from scratch) and the prognosticators (the self-proclaimed experts at prediction of success and failure). James told me the story of a well-known industry observer who took one look at the Baileys idea, and proclaimed, "that shit will never sell." Well, the forecast was wrong, but never mind; that gent went on to make millions in the industry anyhow.

[After this story was posted, the gentleman contacted me and told me I had it backwards. He claims he said this shit will *sell.]*

Jerry Mann told me a story about Bailey's right after I took over new products. His advice began with a typical Jerry Mann comment. "Listen pal," he said between puffs, "in this business, you just never know what will sell and what won't."

It seems that when Jerry was running a distributor operation in California, a friend called and asked for a favor, which was to buy some 5,000 cases of a new cream liqueur. He thought it was doomed for failure, but a friend asked for a favor, and Jerry complied. As he put it, "we stuck the crap in the back of the warehouse and forgot all about it." Then one day out of the blue, a sales manager called and informed him that retailers were clamoring for "that crap at the back of the warehouse."

7 million cases annually later, despite ups and downs, lower priced knock-offs, and diet and weight concerns, Baileys is still going strong as a true global brand.

According to James, it was launched using a strategic new product approach; a strong dedicated team, management commitment, and an understanding of consumer needs and wants. This planning gave the brand its momentum. Once you get momentum, boys and girls, even a large bureaucratic behemoth can't slow you down.

Coyote Tequila

I was at lunch with an old friend who worked on Seagram new products and packaging design. He reminded me of the Coyote Tequila story, and the supremacy of product over imagery. It is also a story of how logic and formulae don't work in new product development.

When I was running new products, the single-minded goal was to fill holes in the overall portfolio. There was no larger hole than the absence of tequila.

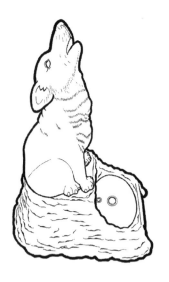

Oh sure, there were two wannabe brands in the company's history. One was Olmeca and the other was Mariachi, both now owned by Pernod Ricard. I'm not sure how well or poorly they are doing now, but at the time, they were in the "brand hospice" division of Seagram. So the mission was to create a tequila brand that could compete with the dominant Jose Cuervo, in a category that at the time, showed incredible promise. (This was pre-Patron.)

The project was launched with gusto, intensity, and the best team and intentions. No effort was spared; no resource (in or out of the company) was held back; it was full steam ahead.

The first step on the journey was to develop a concept; one that could make the new brand stand out from the others on the market, and perhaps do for tequila what Captain Morgan did for rum. After all, it was argued, Bacardi dominates rum much the same way as Cuervo does tequila, and the extra added attraction of a flavored product could separate the new tequila from the rest. Hmmm... sounded logical to me.

But what's the name and imagery? Coyote, of course... as in southwest, as in rough and tough, as in sneaks up on you and steals your cattle, as in—you get the picture.

To further borrow a page from the Captain Morgan playbook, a howling pedestal was conceived and produced for bars. Each time a bottle was taken off the pedestal, a button was released, and that activated the sound of a howling Coyote. The trade loved it. It reminded all of us of the highly successful Captain mirrors that bars clamored for. It cost a bloody fortune— but who cared, this was Seagram, and we're taking on tequila. We'll make it up on volume, as the saying goes.

Now for the formulation. What we learned was that most people at the time thought the taste of tequila was awful, and that's why the Margarita was invented. For the rest, the awful taste was a badge of machismo courage that would be forgotten after a few rounds of shots. Oh, and let's not forget the salt and lime ritual.

As a result, someone in Research & Development (R&D) came up with the notion that Coyote needed to be harsh, a taste that replicated the southwest concept and was truly macho, as in fiery. So this "tequila with natural flavors" was "spiced" with hot peppers. Might have been a billion on the Scoville chili peppers heat scale, for all I know. Whatever, it was doomed from the outset. I can't blame R&D as much as the marketing team and myself for jumping to the wrong conclusion and letting this happen.

On the one hand, we had consumers and the trade loving the idea and the brand. That is, until they tasted it. No matter how hard we tried to get the heat down, it still tasted like crap, and over time the damage was done.

Lessons learned: What works in one instance doesn't necessarily work in another. There are no formulas to success in spirits marketing—or in any category, for that matter. Furthermore, no matter how good the packaging, name, and proposition is, if it tastes awful, it's doomed. Remember the expression "pitting lipstick on a pig." Unless, of course, an awful taste is the concept.

By the way, Seagram never really got tequila right. In addition to Olmeca, Mariachi and Coyote, there were ill-fated efforts with Herradura and Patron. The last attempt, Margaritaville, had promise; but ended when the lights went out.

*   *   *

The mistake we made with Coyote was the assumption that because the leading brand at the time was perceived as tasting awful, it needed to be masked with lime and salt or in a margarita. That led us to believe that the key was to make harsh-

tasting tequila. Wrong. Patron ~~was super successful because it~~ went the other way—a tequila that tasted good and was smooth.

My friend Eileen Higgins, with whom I worked both at Seagram and Jose Cuervo International, pointed out to me that Cuervo's taste profile is sweet and tastes pretty good, yet consumers perceived that it was a rough, machismo taste. That led consumers to drink it, but feel rugged and virile while doing it. Perception versus reality. Even savvy marketers can be fooled.

*　*　*

Tequila and I do not get along.

The first time ~~I tasted tequila when I was in college,~~ I thought I was drinking gasoline. I stayed away from it, and didn't try it again until I got to Seagram and had no choice but to try it, and come up with a meaningful brand.

"DOES THIS HALIBUT TASTE LIKE TEQUILA TO YOU?"

So when I ran new products, that was mission number one. For a while, each Friday morning, we would go up to the new products lab in Westchester to sample various types of tequilas, both flavored and unflavored. Do you have any idea how awful straight tequila tastes at 8:30 in the morning? Oh sure, we had spittoons and we weren't swallowing the stuff, but the taste lingered in my mouth the entire day. Sometimes that night at dinner I could still taste the tequila. (By the way, I was never any good at using a spittoon. More often than not I'd end up dribbling on my tie or shirt.)

Anyhow, we finally ended up with Coyote, and you just read how that turned out.

Next came Patron tequila, and a partnership with John Paul DeJoria and the late Martin Crowley. Seagram grew the brand from 5,000 cases to 50,000 in a short period of time, and despite Mr. Crowley's good intentions, he seemed determined to undermine our sales and marketing efforts. Ultimately the relationship ended in a bitter lawsuit. That's a story for another time. Let's just say it was ugly.

Next was Margaritaville tequila and Jimmy Buffett. You'll read about that in Chapter 7. This one had great potential, but unfortunately, Seagram closed before that happened.

After Seagram, I consulted with my friend Carlos Arana, who ran Jose Cuervo International (JCI) owned by the Beckmann family. In the eight years Carlos ran the business, he grew the brand (in spite of the overwhelming competition from Patron) in revenue, sales, and market share. He literally put Cuervo on the global map. Not long thereafter he left, and so did I.

After that, I was briefly involved with the launch of Avión tequila. For many reasons, I dropped out, and the brand seems to be showing some promise. All I can say is I'm not sorry I moved on.

I guess you can understand why tequila and I don't get along. The only thing I hate more than tequila are confidentiality agreements.

*   *   *

What makes a winner?

Understanding how a brand becomes successful, especially in the alcohol industry, is difficult and elusive. Earlier, I said that it depends on vision, tenacity, and the trade. Let's also add luck to the mix. (And let's not forget the old adage that "luck is the byproduct of hard work." Although I prefer "luck is where opportunity meets preparation.")

In this chapter, we also saw that in the liquor industry, where the imagery versus taste battle rages to determine what makes a winner. Unless it's "in the bottle," no amount of self-perception or imagery can overcome an unpleasant tasting product. That was the Coyote situation. Hold on, you say, what about Jägermeister—wasn't that successful despite the taste? I don't think so; I believe the harsh taste fit the image/perception of the brand.

If there were a rule as to what makes a brand or new product successful, I would say it's the confluence of consumer and trade belief that the brand is both unique and relevant. Jägermeister grew because it had both when it was launched; today, other 'shot' brands have pushed its relevance aside. Captain Morgan had both; Grey Goose and Absolut, in their day, had both; Patron still has both; Crown Royal had uniqueness, but lost its relevance; many of the craft whiskies on the market today are tapping into the craft and whiskey trends (relevant), but only a handful are unique.

Let's look at today's hottest-selling brands to further illustrate the point. Three winners at the moment are: Tito's Handcrafted Vodka, Rumchata, and Fireball Whiskey.

Tito's is growing rapidly by tapping into the craft trend, Americana, and having an attractive price point. Leaving aside my confusion as to how you can call yourself "handcrafted" at over a million cases per year (I think they turn the machines on by hand), it is clearly relevant to consumer wants—but is it unique? While fans of the brand say it is, come on... it's vodka. In this case, the imagery has surpassed the copycat nature of the category.

Rumchata is rum-based cream liqueur that tastes, well, yummy. Actually, it's made with Rum and Horchata, a Latin American drink with a milky appearance and taste. Women in particular seem to love the product, and I've often heard it described as rum with the leftover milk from a sweetened cereal. The taste is unique, and its relevance comes from the allure of cream-based products like Bailey's.

Finally, Fireball has many things going for it. First and foremost is the trend toward shots that started way back with the boilermaker (shot and a beer) (See Old Breed story in chapter 2). More recently, many brands moved into this space, including Jaeger, Jameson, shot drinks like the Slippery Nipple, Car Bomb, and others. So Fireball, a mainly shot-consumed product, fits right in, and its strong cinnamon taste provides both essential elements for success. The shot phenomenon has come back stronger and more unique than the boilermaker.

Let's not forget the concept of "pre-gaming" as an important drinking experience. I like to think of it as doing shots with friends at home before going out drinking. I also think of the shot market as the "economy of the buzz." If you are out drinking with your buddies, it takes lots of beer to get to where you all want to be, and it's expensive. A pre-game shot allows you to coast and not break the bank.

*   *   *

Taking the Goodness Out

In my experience, there are two corporate enemies of brands that can inhibit their growth—production and finance. Two examples:

At a meeting with a plant manager responsible for the production of Seagram's 7 Crown, he told me that if we removed the large embossed '7' on the back of the bottle, he could speed up the production. "Why?" I asked him. Turns out that occasionally, the embossed logos hit each other as they go down the line, and some breakage occurs, causing the line to be stopped. "I can increase production if you remove the embossing." My answer was no. Seagram's 7 was a powerhouse brand once upon a time, and to further denigrate the brand's image would accelerate its death. Whatever cost savings would occur by lessening the breakage and speeding up production would be more than set off by giving the consumer the wrong message.

The other example involves Crown Royal and its bag, which was expensive to produce. But that bag was a major piece of the brand's equity. No one else had such packaging at the time. It made a statement.

That bag had a life long after the contents of the bottle were consumed. It was used to store everything, from jewelry to stashes; people even made clothing and bedspreads out of it. To remove the bag was to remove an important component of the Crown Royal experience. Yet each year at budget time, the production, finance, and outside consultants clamored for its demise.

Fortunately, they never won.

*   *   *

Lessons Learned

What I've learned about brands and brand building in the alcohol industry over the years is applicable to all businesses, but especially those where imagery is a critical component. To me, brand imagery is how the brand makes you look and feel, based on the impression in the consumer's mind of what the brand is all about.

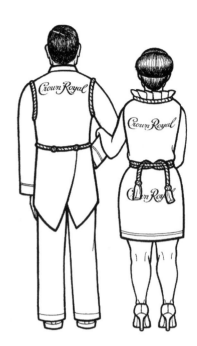

In alcohol, the brand selection is often based on mood, occasion, and situation, from among a set of brands that are considered. The same is true for cosmetics and fragrances, restaurant choice, food brands, and a host of other businesses.

Here's what I've learned about brands and brand building:

- It's about people—their commitment and motivation; their willingness to take risks and think outside the box; their patience and tenacity.

- Analytics—measurements that guide, not rule.

- Sound strategic thinking, including line extensions that "feed the brand, not eat it."

- Strive for uniqueness and relevance.

- Integrated marketing is the key—a unified and seamless experience for consumers in communications; all elements of the marketing mix have to be in sync and work with each other.

- Imagery and intangible benefits must be balanced with product efficacy.

- In the brand adoption model, customer retention is the most important return on investment.

4. Advertising and Beyond—Gentle (and not so gentle) persuasions

We've seen some of the key elements in brand building, including the size of the market (small), key success drivers (patience, instincts, and people), getting through the gates, the bartender, luck, and a host of other factors.

It's not just about advertising. In fact, in brand building, I've often thought about communications in terms of Above the Line (ATL) and Below the Line (BTL). The term originated in the 1950s, when Procter and Gamble (P&G) decided to pay different commissions to agencies engaged in ATL activities, such as mass advertising, as opposed to those who handled promotions and related activity.

From my standpoint, the nature of the liquor business means that traditional mass advertising is not as effective as it is in other consumer packaged goods businesses. However, the digital age plus content marketing and social media have changed the communication landscape in all categories.

To be more precise, a spirits marketer spending millions to run a campaign on TV and in print will not get the same bang for his buck as he would with a web ad or video that goes viral. In many cases, other forms of communication—social media, PR, point of sale, sales incentive programs, direct marketing—make more sense to me.

Look at it this way: given the relatively small size of the spirits drinking population, not everyone who sees an ad in a magazine or on a TV show is a drinker, or a potential drinker. But anyone who goes into a liquor store or the spirits and wine section of a supermarket is much more likely to be a consumer. In fact, if you look closely at the emerging top brands, you'll find that heavy advertising expenditures are unlikely to be at the heart of their developing success.

Let's start with the fun world of advertising, and then move beyond it.

*   *   *

A warning to ad agency executives from the head of a large agency in the 1960s:

"To all employees: If you must drink during lunch, please drink whiskey. It is much better for our clients to know that you are drunk rather than think you are stupid."

*   *   *

Bill Bernbach

There is a great story about Bill Bernbach, Edgar M. Bronfman, and Chivas Regal.

Before I get into it, for those of you who are unfamiliar with Bill, here is the man who revolutionized creativity in advertising—no, make that brand and product selling.

Bill Bernbach's style of advertising changed brand communication. He was the anti-*Mad Men*, focusing on compelling messages that broke through the clutter and resonated with consumers. "The difference between the forgettable and the endurable is artistry," was how he put it. So think about such ads as Avis "We Try Harder," or Volkswagen "Think Small," or "You don't have to be Jewish to love Levy's real Jewish rye bread."

His effort on behalf of Chivas Regal is an interesting story, as described by Edgar M. Bronfman in his book *Good Spirits*, and by Paul Pacult in *A*

Double Scotch—How Chivas Regal and The Glenlivet Became Global Icons.

In the 1960s, after the acquisition of Chivas, the brand began to languish in the face of competition from such lighter scotches as Cutty Sark and J&B Rare. Edgar managed to convince his father (Sam Bronfman) that changes needed to be made to stem the sales declines. These included product reformulation, new packaging, and a new ad campaign. Enter Bill Bernbach.

As the story goes, when Bernbach showed the new candidate ads to Edgar, there was one ad at the bottom of the pile that he kept hiding. When pushed by Bronfman to reveal it, Bernbach pointed out that it was intended as an introductory ad for the new package, and that he was concerned Edgar wouldn't dare run it.

The headline read "What Idiot Changed the Chivas Regal Package?" To his credit, Bronfman saw the benefits of the brashness and self-mocking tone, and to make a long story short, the ad ran.

The team at Doyle, Dane and Bernbach went on to change the brand's fortune by understanding consumers and reaching them through challenges and taunts that were fun and resonated well. My favorite: "If you can't taste the difference in Chivas Regal, save the extra two dollars." And the classic, "The Chivas Regal of Scotches."

In addition to the central print campaign, the agency created a cartoon campaign that picked up on the theme. A particularly memorable one showed a ship leaving the dock with a case of Chivas left behind. The caption read, "They'll be back. They forgot the Chivas."

Did the creativity translate into brand sell? According to the Pacult book, when DDB took over in 1962, the brand was selling around 135,000 cases. By 1979, sales had risen to 1.1 million.

All I can close with is a rewording of another great Bernbach ad: "Mamma mia, that's effective advertising."

Advertising: Creativity

"If it doesn't sell, it isn't creative." David Ogilvy (Ogilvy &Mather)

"In the modern world of business, it is useless to be a creative, original thinker unless you can also sell what you create." David Ogilvy.

Is creativity in brand communication getting better, getting worse, or staying the same?

Ad agency execs will tell you that creativity is alive and well, and that memorable and effective advertising is as relevant today as it was in the past. They will also add that the fragmentation of media creates an environment whereby delivering a highly effective message is diffused and expensive. And the new media options (digital) require new forms of creativity.

The detractors will take the view that the demise of mainstream media has hurt creativity, but not as much as the changes in the advertising business itself. They point out that only small, independent shops can replicate the talent of the past. The large agencies are too busy worrying about overhead and financials to concentrate on the quality of the work.

An ad agency executive friend of mine, who sold his shop to one of the conglomerates, tells the story of an annual agency-wide meeting a few years ago:

All the company Presidents were asked to report on the activities of their business unit. Speaker after speaker—from New York to New Delhi—talked about revenues, profitability, new business development, overhead, etc. Finally one exec from a highly creative firm couldn't stand it anymore and got up and shouted, "Are we ever going to talk about the fucking work we produce?"

Finally, a most appropriate quote from David Ogilvy:

Many people—and I think I am one of them—are more productive when they've had a little to drink. I find if I drink two or three brandies, I'm far better able to write.

Couldn't have said it better myself.

*　　*　　*

For me, the relationship with an ad agency is about the creativity and the skill of the art directors and copywriters. The other members of an agency team are important, but at the end of the day, it is the "message" that the client is buying. At Seagram, we had an in-house media department, and it was the role of brand managers to develop strategies and plans. As a result, any assistance from the ad agency in these areas was superfluous. As far as account executives are concerned, I can buy my own lunch.

It's about the work; which is probably why more and more clients are moving away from 'agency of record' to a project-based approach.

My friend and favorite creative director, Bill Berenter of BgTwo and co-founder of the ad agency Berenter, Greenhouse, Webster, has an interesting view of the evolution of the advertising industry. He points out that in the last 50 years, there have been four stages.

Prior to the 1960s, the agency business was based on the old boys' network, and also largely on where you went to school. Relationships were more important than the work itself. As Mad Men *has chronicled, the next era was the "kingdom of the creative" and the power of the message. That gave way in the 1990s to agency conglomerates, and the importance of the stock price and Wall Street scrutiny. Today, the business is seeing a return to the quality of the work (message), and there is a reluctance to pay for overhead and long-term commitments. So there is a return to the power of creativity. Hooray!*

*   *   *

Advertising – The Client

Two of my favorite quotes about advertising:

"Every advertisement should be thought of as a contribution to the complex symbol, which is the brand image." David Ogilvy (O&M)

"I have always believed that writing advertisements is the second most profitable form of writing. The first, of course, is ransom notes..." Phil Dusenberry (BBDO ad agency)

Years ago, when I was in marketing research, my good friend who was the CEO of a midsized company asked me to conduct some focus groups on a new campaign his ad agency had developed. After doing the work, I came back with the recommendation that he proceed; the message was in line with the strategy, and consumers liked the creative effort.

He kept challenging me on each and every positive insight I shared with him. Finally, in exasperation, I asked my friend/client what the problem was. He looked at me and said, "Arthur, there is nothing you can tell me that will change how I feel. I hate the campaign." "So why did you bother hiring me to test it?" I asked. "I was hoping consumers would hate it as well. Now I'll just kill it on my own."

Our debate continued. "What don't you like about it?" I asked him. "I just don't like it," was the reply. "Why not give your agency some guidelines for what you're looking for?"

"Listen," he said, "I'll know good advertising when I see it."

It's good to be the CEO.

When Stupidity Overtakes Creativity

Here is a lesson in how not to do advertising.

Wódka vodka, an inexpensive import trying to become the next Svedka, stepped on it's you-know-what with an outdoor message that it obviously (but mistakenly) thought was cute and clever.

Some time ago, they ran a billboard in New York City with this sophomoric content: "Christmas Quality, Chanukah Pricing." That ran into a firestorm of criticism, and they had to literally pull the ads down.

You'd think they would have learned and moved forward in a number of new ways to get their message across. Get a new creative team, hire a new agency, and/or get internal marketing and advertising people who know what they are doing. There are dozens of ways to get the quality-low price message across in a fun or even shocking way, without being offensive.

But the next time they ran a billboard with "Escort Quality, Hooker Pricing." The best I can say for it is that it's lame. But to compound matters, they chose to run the ad on the Bruckner Expressway (trying to reach Westchester commuters) in the Hunts Point section of the Bronx. According to the *Daily News*, "When I saw it I almost fell out of my seat," said Rafael Salamanca Jr., district manager for CB 2 (local Community Board). "That's an inappropriate billboard given what the Hunts Point community has gone through in the past."

Some advice for the managers at Wódka's marketing company: Outdoor advertising and alcohol have always been on tenuous grounds, and this is not a good thing for your brand or for the industry. The childishness of the ad is not worth the effort.

The genius who loves this campaign will probably say something about how even negative publicity is good publicity. Well, that's not always the case; especially when there are competitive brands with more positive messages than "buy me, I'm cheap."

As far as the outdoor company is concerned—shame on you for allowing this to go up. That company used to have high standards and community sensitivity. I guess an ad about hookers fits their current business practices.

By the way... Wódka's sales today are still very low. That's what happens when you mess with the universe.

*   *   *

The ad campaign for Wódka was derived from earlier efforts around the idea/ad known as, "Dress British, Think Yiddish."

Barry Popik has a webite called "The Big Apple," and I found this there:

"Dress British, Think Yiddish" is cited from at least 1962 and means to look conventional, but to think unconventionally. The phrase (also given as "Look British, Think Yiddish" and "Speak British, Think Yiddish") was printed on buttons in the 1960s. Saint Laurie Ltd., a men's clothier in New York, used "Dress British, Think Yiddish" in a 1980s advertising campaign.

*   *   *

"What did the client say?"

I came across an interesting and amusing piece in *Ad Age Daily* I wanted to share, in case you haven't seen it.

Derek Walker, whom I've never met but hope to meet someday, has a blog about advertising. He describes himself as "the janitor, secretary and mailroom person" for his tiny agency, Brown and Browner advertising, based in Columbia, S.C. So right off the bat, I like him.

His posting in *Ad Age* was called, "Clients Say the Funniest Things." Since I've been on both sides of the desk, I found his client quotes and reactions to advertising creatives to be right on target and very funny.

So to those of you on the agency side, please enjoy. Those of you on the client side, well, here's what some of your counterparts elsewhere, ahem...

sound like. For those of you who haven't witnessed the presentation of creative messages and the reactions, this will be a window on the dance that sometimes takes place.

WE LOVE THE CONCEPT, IT'S GREAT! BUT CAN WE CHANGE THE VISUAL, REWORK THE HEADLINE, AND ADJUST THE COPY? OTHER THAN THAT, WE LOVE IT!

Here's the ironic part: these reactions often happen to marketers themselves, when they present creative work to their management—who, in effect, is a client.

EVERYONE LOVED THE CONCEPT, THEN I TOOK IT HOME AND SHOWED IT TO MY WIFE WHO USED TO BE AN ENGLISH TEACHER, AND SHE SAID THE LINE ISN'T GRAMMATICALLY CORRECT. CAN YOU WRITE A NEW HEADLINE?

With thanks to Derek Walker for his approval, here are some client comments he has heard:

I SURE MISS THE DAYS WHEN ALL WE HAD TO DO WAS PRODUCE A CALENDAR WITH TITS AND ASS AND EVERYONE WAS HAPPY.

- We love the concept, it's great! But can we change the visual, rework the headline, and adjust the copy? Other than that, we love it!"

- "We don't want 'friends' or for people to 'like' us. We want customers."

- "In the marketing class I took in college, the instructor said you should mention your company's name at least seven times in a radio spot to be effective. Can we add 5 more mentions? That would make it great."

- On social media: "I get it, but I'm worried that people will start talking about our product without us."

- After laughing hilariously for a couple of moments: "That's great! It does everything we want and it stands out. But seriously, let's see the real work."

- "Everyone loved the concept, then I took it home and showed it to my wife who used to be an English teacher, and she said the line isn't grammatically correct. Can you write a new headline?"

- "I don't understand why you put in so much effort. It's only a website. Couldn't we just throw up something and be done with it?"

- "Do we really need to be creative? I mean, isn't our product great enough to attract attention?"

- "I don't believe in advertising, we're only doing this because our competitors are."

- "I sure miss the days when all we had to do was produce a calendar with tits and ass and everyone was happy."

For some of us in the **Booze Business**, the last one really resonates.

*   *   *

Now for the other side of communications...

Product Placements

Think about *E.T.* and Reese's Pieces. Various vodkas and James Bond. *You've Got Mail* and Starbucks.

Product placements in film and TV, depending on whom you talk to, are considered a critical brand building or reinforcement tool. There are some, however, who see it as low impact—it's ok, if you don't have to pay for it.

Consider this from a study on the subject in *Cognitive Daily*: "Product placements in movies: When they work, and when they don't."

...The type of product-placement an advertiser opts for should depend on their marketing goals. If you want to build awareness ... it's probably best to opt for a placement that plays a role in the story itself. But if you just want to reinforce preferences for a well-known brand (say, "Coke" versus "Pepsi"), it's probably not necessary to go to that expense. Just having your brand in the movie works just as well.

My first exposure to product placement (albeit from a distance) came shortly after I joined Seagram. It was on behalf of Herradura Tequila.

Based on film industry connections, the company had an opportunity (which I believe turned into a mandate) to place the brand in a film called *Tequila Sunrise*. Aside from the title as a perfect fit, the placement involved brand exposure galore; verbal mentions, bottle exposure on the bar, and being consumed by the actors, signage, even a bus passing by with a

Herradura ad on the side. So there was a role for the brand in the story—not a central role—but the title alone made the brand a key element.

Furthermore, *Tequila Sunrise* was star-studded, and sure to have target audience appeal. Mel Gibson, Michelle Pfeiffer, and Kurt Russell starred; Robert Towne wrote and directed the movie. A sure thing, right?

The movie sucked, and never lived up to its promise. A *Variety* review summed it up nicely: "There's not much kick in this cocktail, despite its mix of quality ingredients." Roger Ebert wrote, "It's hard to surrender yourself to a film that seems to be toying with you."

The small number of people who saw the film agreed.

I've always been a proponent of product placement and integration. To me, it makes good sense as a brand-building tool. But I've learned the following:

- Positive impact on a brand is not a foregone conclusion. No matter how well the product is shown and integrated, sometimes the only winner is the TV or film producer.

- For adult beverages, how the product is portrayed is as important as the portrayal itself. Enough said.

- If the story doesn't click with audiences, the brand becomes "collateral damage." Unfortunately, there's no real way to predict it—but it's worth the shot.

Have you noticed what *E.T.* did for Reese's Pieces? As I've been told, it was first offered to Mars on behalf of M&M's, and they turned it down. Hershey said yes.

Keepers of the Quaich

A Quaich (pronounced "kwayx") is the classic small drinking bowl of Scotland, and the centerpiece of this story.

The Keepers of the Quaich is a Scotch whisky society with membership by invitation only. James Espey founded it, along with several others, to acknowledge those who have contributed to the Scotch whisky industry.

James has held very senior positions in the liquor industry, including at United Distillers, International Distillers, and Vintners, Seagram, and others. He's known for the creation of Bailey's and Malibu, among other brands, and is the consummate marketing and managerial professional.

He also has a great sense of humor, so it comes as no surprise that he would help found a 500-year-old society in 1988.

Everything about the society and its induction process is serious and worthwhile, but in my humble opinion, it's also a hoot, especially the stories surrounding the event and ceremony.

On the serious side, while I'm not sure how it works today, the people who ran the society when I was inducted put on a great event. The Keepers had its own tartan, and inductees received a cummerbund made in that plaid. There is a coat of arms with the motto *Uisgebeatha Gu Brath* which means "The Water of Life For Ever."

The event itself is held at Blair Castle, the ancient home and fortress of the Earls and Dukes of Atholl. The ceremony, as I recall it, was something to behold—even for the most blasé "been there and done it" **Booze Business** executive.

Throughout the induction ceremony and the serious and splendid dinner, you feel honored and totally enthralled by the evening. It isn't until the end of the meal, when the inductees are full of Scotch and haggis, and standing on the tables singing, that one realizes this is just good fun.

About the standing on the table bit: perhaps some readers who are members could enlighten me as to the number of injuries that have occurred over the years when tables collapsed. My memory is a bit hazy on that aspect of the evening. I recall standing and singing a Scottish drinking song, and vaguely remember joining everyone else as we stood on the chairs and raised our voices. But how the few hundred others got on the tables to end the song is beyond my recollection.

Ah, and the haggis. Now there's a tale, laddie.

As the dinner began, two men appeared, one holding the haggis and the other looking like he had come from central casting. With a booming voice, the second man recited the Robert Burns poem *Address to a Haggis*. Allow me to set the stage for you.

As you remember from high school, Robert Burns was a renowned Scottish poet and lyricist, widely regarded as the national poet of Scotland.

Haggis is a dish containing sheep's liver, lungs, and heart mixed with onion, salt, oatmeal, and other stuff, that's simmered and served in a sheep's stomach. Let's just say that like Scotch, it's an acquired taste. (The term "mystery meat" you used in high school doesn't begin to describe it.)

The poem is a celebration of the dish's role as a unique and symbolic part of the Scottish identity and culture. So it's more than fitting that the Keeper's dinner should begin with this presentation of the haggis, accompanied by the Burns poem.

As the story goes, at one particular induction dinner, things went awry. Picture the server carrying this enormous haggis, followed by the booming voice reciting the poem.

As he walks down the dining room, his voice gets louder when approaching the final verse, the translation of which is:

You powers who make mankind your care

And dish them out their meals

Old Scotland wants no watery food

That splashes in dishes

But if you wish her grateful prayer

Give her a haggis!

Just then, the server slips, and the haggis is tossed four feet in the air. It lands with a loud thud and showers haggis everywhere. We're talking meat and offal on the tables, floors, chandeliers, and a few dozen Keepers in tuxedos with their unique tartan cummerbunds.

At this point, one of the longstanding members was heard to remark: "I see they've added a new element to this year's event...the flying haggis."

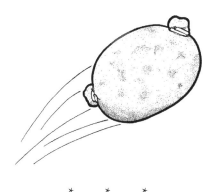

*   *   *

Is it whisky or whiskey?

The difference is this: while there are distinctive spellings products from different countries account for the two different spellings. American and Irish Whiskey; Scotch, Canadian, and Japanese Whisky. As you have noticed, sometimes I get cagey and spell it whisk(e)y.

In case you don't know, the origin of the word goes back to both Ireland and Scotland. Uisge beatha or usquebaugh is Gaelic for "water of life." It was translated from the Latin aqua vitae, used to describe spirits.

*   *   *

The Captain and the Retailer

An east coast retailer persuaded Seagram to hire his son. He started his career like most people: calling on stores during the day, and doing on-premise promotions at night. On this particular night, he was working a Captain Morgan drink night, and since he was the "new guy" he had to wear the captain suit.

It seems he had a bit too much to drink, and in direct violation of company policy, he decided to drive home instead of finding alternate means of transportation. Shortly after leaving the bar, with his reactions a bit dulled from sampling the Captain, he rear-ended the car stopped in front of him at a traffic light. Realizing he was in a bit of trouble, he decided that his best course of action was to get out of there as quickly as possible. He left the car and ran to a nearby business, from which he caught a cab home.

Once safely home, he made another fateful decision, calling the police to report that his car was stolen. This was just about the same time that a police car rolled up to the scene of the accident. When the officer asked the driver of the car that was rear-ended what happened, he said he wasn't really sure, but the guy driving the car that hit him was dressed as a pirate and ran away.

As you can imagine, it didn't take long for law enforcement to figure out what happened. A few days later, the young Seagram recruit was back working behind the counter at his family's liquor store.

*   *   *

Digital Marketing and Social Media

When I ran marketing at Seagram, despite the very large budget I had to work with, I still felt that major expenditures on mass advertising were wasteful. I believed I could get more bang for the buck with PR, with point of sale and other promotions. If I were still there, I would be putting the overwhelming amount of the communication budget into those efforts, plus social media and related digital marketing.

Let's look at it this way. If a filmed advertisement costs $5 million to produce, you still have to spend a ton of money for distribution via networks, cable, and other paid media; perhaps as much as an additional $10-15 million to reach the intended audience. But in the digital age, assuming you have a clever or noteworthy ad, the consumer will find you.

From the *Financial Times*, August 2015:

Digital marketing is an umbrella term for the targeted, measurable, and interactive marketing of products or services using digital technologies to reach and convert leads into customers. The key objective is to promote brands, build preference and increase sales through various digital marketing techniques. It is embodied by an extensive selection of service, product and brand marketing tactics, which mainly use the Internet as a core promotional medium, in addition to mobile and traditional TV and radio.

Other people may have invented the Internet, but my team at Seagram and I jumped all over it. In fact, Captain Morgan was a distant second to Bacardi, and while they were sleeping, we registered rum.com. To this day, if you go to that URL, the Captain Morgan site comes up. In an industry where the target audience is limited in size, and the ability to reach them, it was clear that mastery of digital marketing was—and still is—vital.

Print and broadcast advertising—in other words, mass media—can be wasteful. The cost involves casting a wide net, but the results often limited. Remember the "size of the market" remarks I made in Chapter 1? It was clear to us in the early 1990s that given limited budgets, we could not afford to spend as much as it would take to make an impact in any mass medium. Enter direct marketing; or as some back in the day referred to it, direct mail marketing.

What we did was build a database, partly by acquiring lists of spirits drinkers, and mainly by getting names from consumers who applied for rebates (coupons), a common brand incentive at point-of-sale at the time. It wasn't always just about getting money back; it often involved a t-shirt or hat, barware or glasses, or some other premium item. By the time Seagram was sold, there was an enormous database worth millions. Therefore, unsurprisingly, with the advent of the Internet, the economics and the power of direct marketing changed appreciably. Additionally, loyalty and consumer relationship management (CRM) tools entered the marketing mix.

Fast forward to social media today. In a July 2015 article on the top 10 spirits brands on social media, *The Spirits Business*, an online industry newsletter, had this to say:

Social media is not just a useful tool, it's necessary for striking up direct communication with a target audience, engaging them and ultimately translating that engagement into further brand loyalty.

By the way, their number one choice for the best social media user was Stolichnaya. Over 5.3 million fans on Facebook, 114,000 Twitter followers, and nearly 21,000 Instagram followers.

It's not just about the social media outlets. YouTube, UPROXX, Vox, Hulu, even Facebook have become outlets for branded content (also known as branded entertainment). Fanscape, a leading social media marketing agency, defines branded content as follows:

Branded entertainment encompasses any piece of content (scripted or unscripted, comedy or drama, series or one-off) that is made with a brand's personality, positioning and marketing objectives in mind. Branded entertainment has the brand's essence baked into the core of the content idea.

Some examples include Marriott's *Two Bellmen* (an action-comedy about two bellmen who prove their company loyalty by battling thieves), or Chipotle's *Farmed and Dangerous*. Here are two from the spirits world:

- Jim Beam – "Bold Choices" campaign encouraged fans to use Facebook to share stories of the bold choices they had made in their lives. To get into the spirit of the campaign, Fred Noe—Jim Beam's great grandson and master distiller— promised he would get a Jim Beam tattoo if the brand got one million friends on Facebook. He did.

- Jack Daniel's – "The Independence Project" is a storytelling approach to social media, instead of a selling approach. They asked fans to submit videos describing their own independent project—the freedom Americans have to turn their dreams into reality—was the theme.

What I find so interesting is that in the 1950s, television took off because companies like Proctor and Gamble and Lever Brothers wanted a way to utilize the new medium to promote their brands. So they created soap operas. It seems to me that this new digital world is doing the same.

*   *   *

Tying the pieces together...

The brand building battle relies on communications, and most people think this includes advertising. But I like the idea (paraphrasing Vince Lombardi), that advertising is everything, but it's not the only thing. There is a role and place for each element in the marketing mix.

Consider the consumer brand adoption model:

Awareness > Familiarity > Trial > Usage > Adoption > Retention (Loyalty)

Each step in the process can be addressed by a number of different types of communications, not just advertising. Awareness can be built in a number of ways, including advertising, social media, word of mouth, product placement, etc. Familiarity and Trial are probably best in the domain of sampling and other point of purchase elements. I could go on and on, but I think you get the picture. Each element of communications has a role (sometimes multiple roles) on the pathway from awareness to loyalty. The key, however, is that each element has to work in tandem with the others, and above all, must be in harmony with the other elements. Sometimes referred to as "integrated marketing," it is the holistic approach to communication in marketing. It involves consistency both in the marketplace and online; making sure that consumers understand the message; and ensuring that all elements work together with the same tone, manner, and voice.

5. Shakers and Stirrers—What does it take to succeed?

"I GOT SUCCESSFUL BECAUSE I'M LUCKY. BUT I DIDN'T GET LUCKY UNTIL I STARTED WORKING 80 HOURS A WEEK."

I don't know whether it's because of my blog, my consulting practice, or longevity in the **Booze Business**, but hardly a week goes by without my being contacted by a wannabe alcohol industry mogul. Perhaps it's the desire to be the next Sidney Frank (creator of Grey Goose), or maybe because it's seen as an easy way to become a successful entrepreneur. Neither is viable.

A typical conversation starts with 1) An amazing product idea that was served to friends and relatives who absolutely love it 2) There's nothing like it on the market or 3) I came across this product in East Jabulya and I want to import it. My favorite was the gentleman who told me his grandmother passed away and left him $100,000, and he wanted to use the money to start a liquor business—a noble ideal, but that's not nearly enough money to even get started.

Of course, there are startups that gain traction, and even succeed. You will meet some of these more worthwhile ventures and the people behind them in this chapter. Many of them have worked very hard, overcome enormous challenges, and are still not out of the woods. The obstacles? Of course, money and other resources are a prime ingredient of success, but there are other forces at work.

The alcohol industry, particularly spirits, has contracted (think oligopoly) with consolidated and very powerful suppliers, and a handful of distributors. Oh and let's not forget Mr. Retailer; whose first question, when presented with a new product, will very likely be, "which of the brands on the shelf that are *already* selling do you want me to take down to make room for your new product/brand?"

Think of the other important gatekeeper—the distributor sales rep. He/she has an enormous book of brands, and a livelihood to maintain. He/she can push known brands (often on promotion) that are desired by the trade, or they can "hand sell" the new product no one ever heard of, much less tasted. In the amount of time it takes to sell a case of a startup brand, they could be selling a hand truck of popular vodka. What would you do, if you were a sales rep?

Yet despite the uphill battles, startups *do* succeed. Craft beers are changing the face of the beer industry; similarly, craft distillers are making their mark in the spirits world. You need not look further than the big boys in liquor and beer, who see the handwriting on the wall and have rushed to join the "craft" or "small batch" parade. As Jackie Summers of Sorel Liqueur (who you will meet soon) likes to say—there's a difference between "craft" and "crafty."

Let's meet some of the startups I've gotten to know, and discuss the challenges this new breed of alcohol industry entrepreneurs face.

By the way, regardless of all this, if you want to talk about a startup or new booze product, feel free to contact me.

* * *

Startups

Ever since Sidney Frank sold Grey Goose in 2005 for billions of dollars, the industry has attracted many entrepreneurs with the dream of inventing a brand, building it, flipping it, and moving on to the next one.

It's a good thing. The growth of an industry, any industry, depends on the infusion of new ideas, capabilities, and fresh passion. Look at the rising stars, fast track and hot brands of the industry. You'll find lots of entrepreneurial and startup brands.

But for every winner, there are loads of wannabes with eyes bigger than their stomachs. An investment banker friend described it to me this way:

Almost every week I get a guy coming in, generally in his 30's, who made some money in some type of entrepreneurial venture, was out drinking with his buddy, and the two of them decide they can do this…build a winner. It's usually vodka with an over-the-top package, a half-baked story, and they say they're out every night pushing the brand. Most of the time I think that they use the brand and their "ownership" to impress the ladies.

There's a rule in new product development that I've mentioned before: a winning idea needs to be unique and relevant. To succeed, a brand also needs to be both.

Also luck—the byproduct of hard work.

Want to start your own liquor company?

Go to Moonshine University. Really.

If you're interested in becoming a chef, you might consider the Culinary Institute of America, so why not consider a school to teach you the craft of making liquor? Well, there is such a school. It's part of Distilled Spirits Epicenter.

The first stop in becoming the next **Booze Business** tycoon is the school.

The Distilled Spirits Epicenter has a number of different businesses to help the wannabe craft distiller. One is called Grease Monkey Distillery, which is designed for use by everyone from entrepreneurs to industry experts, and is equipped to distill spirits of all kinds. Think do-it-yourself, and still using state-of-the-art equipment.

What good is an outstanding, crafted liquid without a vessel to put it in? Well, then avail yourself of Challenge Bottling. It is a highly flexible bottling line that is versatile enough to handle smaller production runs, challenging projects, and various packaging requirements. In other words, they are contract bottlers.

Let's go back to Moonshine U. No, they don't teach you to find a remote spot in the woods, set up a still, cook the mash, and drive like hell to outrun the revenuers.

Instead, they have a fairly comprehensive 5-day program, which I find impressive. The curriculum encompasses learning the fundamentals, the production of rum, whiskey, vodka, and gin, and general management covering all aspects of marketing, sales, and distribution. It isn't cheap ($5,500), but I'm guessing it's well worth the money.

Aside from the aspiring liquor moguls, the school is a good place for marketing and sales people to learn about the liquor business, and see more of the production landscape. At Seagram, we had a similar program at the Lawrenceburg KY plant, which was very popular. Absolut had one in a town called Åhus, Sweden; which was both educational, and afforded the opportunity to eat herring. (Hey, don't laugh—it was world-class herring.)

Seriously, Moonshine University is a very worthwhile endeavor in the heart of the Kentucky. Distilled Spirits Epicenter has an endorsement by virtue of its membership in the Kentucky Distillers' Association as the group's first-ever Educational Distillery member.

About the only thing they don't teach you is how to get lucky and produce a winner. That's up to you.

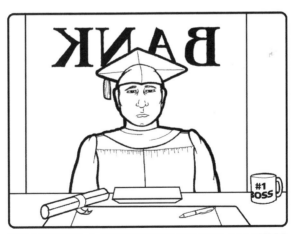

"I'M SORRY, A DEGREE IN BOOZE-MAKING
IS NOT ENOUGH REFERENCE FOR A LOAN."

Brooklyn Booze

Brooklyn is known for many things—churches, the original home of the Dodgers, peculiar accents and pronunciations, the third largest city in the country (if it were a city), and being my "hometown."

It also has an interesting history in the alcohol industry, particularly in distilled spirits.

For one thing, there's Kings County Distillery, which claims to be New York City's oldest operating whiskey distillery, the first since before prohibition. They produce handcrafted bourbon and moonshine (a.k.a. white whiskey).

In doing my research about them, other distillers, and the history of Brooklyn in the **Booze Business**, I came across some interesting information.

In January 2012, the estimated number of micro distiller startups in the U.S. was said to be between 150 and 250 (as of this writing, the number is estimated to be over 600). New York and Oregon are the two leading states. In New York, the state offers a special, inexpensive permit for small-batch distilleries. To get the license, there are application forms, a fee, an interview, and an agreement to source most of the ingredients from New York farmers. The state and the entrepreneurial spirit have revived an industry that was totally destroyed by prohibition.

In addition to Kings County Distillery (bourbon, moonshine, and chocolate whiskey), Brooklyn is also the home of Breuckelen Distilling (gin and whiskey), New York Distilling Co. (rye and gin), Brooklyn Brewery (beer), Industry City Distillery, Widow Jane Distillery, Greenhook Ginsmiths, Red Hook winery (wine), Jack From Brooklyn (which you will read about next), and many others.

Earlier I mentioned the cooperation between government and distillers? It wasn't always that way. Which brings me to the Great Whiskey War of 1869 in Brooklyn, also known as the Moonshine War.

There were dozens, if not scores, of distilleries and rectifiers in Brooklyn around the time of the Civil War. For whatever reason—lawlessness or concern about corruption and misuse of tax dollars—most decided not to pay taxes. We think of moonshiners as living in the rural areas of the south and the Ozarks, but my hometown was right up there with the best of them.

According to a post published on the Brooklyn Library blog: "From 1866 through 1868 the newspapers were full of reports of seized distilleries. In 1867 the government collected only $21,618 from Brooklyn distillers, when in fact the volume of liquor they produced should have yielded $1,225,000 in duties."

By 1869, the revenuers could no longer stand it, and were itching for a fight. So on the morning of December 4, 1869, close to 1,200 troops and a small army of tax collectors were sent into the Fifth Ward of the borough. The area was also known then as "Irish Town," a waterfront district of factories and tenements adjacent to the Navy Yard. Thirteen distilleries were utterly demolished.

Raids involving stills and equipment destruction, and ultimately arrests of the Brooklyn moonshiners, continued throughout the early 1870s. At one raid, as many as 1,500 soldiers were involved. Some of them were observed enjoying the products they confiscated, and were totally inebriated. By 1876, the moonshiners had begun to abandon Brooklyn; some changed professions, and a number moved to Manhattan.

As one historian put it, "The story of Brooklyn moonshiners and their struggle against federal authority is more than a colorful bit of local history. It is the tale...of the extension of the government into the lives of ordinary citizens."

Politics aside, I'm glad that micro distillers are back in Brooklyn.

But the Dodgers can stay where they are.

Jack From Brooklyn

My friend, fellow blogger, and alcohol beverage attorney Robert Lehrman, knowing of my interest in matters dealing with Brooklyn and Booze, introduced me to Jackie Summers. Jack owns a startup business called Jack From Brooklyn (JFB).

Just another startup, you say. That's right—but unlike most, Jackie has the street smarts and entrepreneurial drive to break away from the pack and become a real winner. For those of you who doubt it, as we used to say in Brooklyn, "Wanna bet?"

What Jack has in common with the other micro distilleries, microbrewers, and the like is a presence in a part of New York City that's conducive to new ventures, and also the sense to avail himself of the state's tax and fee incentives.

But Jack From Brooklyn has way more going for it.

Let's start with the product. Unlike all the others, he is not producing an artisanal vodka or whiskey. The product is a brand called Sorel, and it's a liqueur/vodka specialty. In a review in *Wine Enthusiast*, it was referred to it as, "A hibiscus-spiked liqueur that evokes Caribbean spice and sunshine."

Here's how JFB describes Sorel:

The natives of the Caribbean islands have long known the hibiscus plant to be a potent spice. Renown for its curative properties...they would ferment its flowers, and serve on festive occasions. Each island enjoyed slight differences in their recipes, relative to their indigenous horticulture.

It is with great respect for its traditional heritage we present a modern twist on an exotic classic:

The brightness of Brazilian clove. The warmth of Indonesian cassia. The heat of Nigerian ginger. The woody bottom of Indonesian nutmeg. The full, aromatic body of Moroccan hibiscus. Pure cane sugar. The finest 100% organic NY grain alcohol.

I think it tastes great, both as an aperitif and in a cocktail. In fact, Sorel is extremely mixable. I've had it with sparkling wine, vodka, rum, and even whiskey. It's a brand that plays nice with other liquor.

Another interesting aspect of the venture is the smart way Jack has approached marketing and distribution. In New York, a supplier can get a wholesalers' license for their own brand. So instead of being one of a bazillion brands in a salesperson's book, he is master of his own fate. And after hooking up with a delivery company, he's freed up to do the marketing and selling without running all over the city. Told you he was smart.

*   *   *

Update:

I have written about Jackie Summers and Sorel Hibiscus Liqueur on four different occasions since 2012, including the aftermath of Hurricane Sandy and the devastation of Red Hook, Brooklyn. Jackie survived and the brand continued to grow and increase its allure among consumers and bartenders/mixologists. Jackie's story continues and I will be writing about him more on the blog.

For now, Jackie and Sorel (as of this writing) are about to embark on a new and exciting new direction.

*   *   *

From Ballet to Booze

Meet Allison Patel, a whisky-loving woman and former ballerina.

Allison is the owner/producer of her own whisky, Brenne, a French single malt made in Cognac, France. She reinvented herself and entered the **Booze Business** in her second career, after hanging up her tutu and pointe shoes.

And I am very glad that she did—trust me when I tell you it's a terrific, world-class whisky. It's very unique, smooth, and approachable.

Brenne is made from estate-grown barley and is harvested, distilled, matured, and bottled in Cognac, France. The distilling expertise comes from a third generation craft distiller. As Allison describes it, "It's crafted from seed to spirit." The taste is extraordinary, as a result of the malted barley and the barreling. Brenne Whisky starts in new Limousin oak barrels and is finished in Cognac casks, giving it the slight hint of fruit that sets it apart from other whiskies. Each bottle comes from a single barrel selected at its peak. Brenne was officially launched in October 2012, but only after many years of development and maturation of the product. So add patience to Allison's skill set.

Allison's personal story is no less interesting. She and her husband have always shared a passion for international food and drink; making an effort to visit local markets, wineries, and distilleries in their travels, they developed an appreciation of great taste experiences, especially in their favorite category—whisky.

After failing to find many "non-traditional" whiskies in the U.S., Allison took it into her own her hands and started setting up an import/export company. Allison has drive and tenacity, mixed with charm and humility. She launched a brand and still managed to maintain a balanced view of her efforts. One chat with Allison is all it takes to feel great about the future of the spirits industry. From Allison's personal blog, The Whisky Woman, about being a **Booze Business** startup:

> *This is not an easy road at all. Naturally, I only share publicly the highlights of this journey, but I tell people who are thinking about starting their own brand in the spirits world to not be fooled by the happy-go-lucky social media sharing; everything looks easier then it seems, even the stuff that looks impossible. But... the moment when you start to realize your dream is becoming a reality is unlike anything else. It's deep, exciting and can rock you to the core.*

I guess that dancing on your toes is good training for the **Booze Business**.

By the way, Allison often teams up with Jackie Summers and his Sorel Liqueur for joint promotion opportunities. In fact, it was Jack who introduced us, and poured me a Brenne and Sorel cocktail called The Last Call. We're talking amazing here. (Recipe: 2 oz. Brenne, 1 oz. Sorel, let it rest and breath for a minute. Enjoy.)

How a Chilean Wine came to the U.S. via China...and won awards

Don Mateo Wines started with three global entrepreneurs, a passion for winemaking, and a desire to become world-class.

What's so special? There are lots of aspiring winemakers out there.

Yes, but how many have won four awards at a Wine and Spirits Wholesalers of America (WSWA) convention? And how many have had a journey that began in China?

I first met the partners running Don Mateo Wines in late 2010, and was immediately struck by their business acumen, which they gained in global trading and applied to the wine world.

Andy Lam and his brother Matthew were successful exporters of various products and commodities to Chile from China. The currency exchange swings hurt their business over the years, so they turned the ship around and began importing wine from Chile instead. Their passion for wine helped, and they began buying vineyards and wineries. It took patience and tenacity to develop top quality wines. They hit the Chinese wine market at the right point in time, and the business flourished.

You can't be a global wine player without the U.S. market; so Peter Loucks, a third partner, entered the picture and applied his overall business skills to the wine business. Peter is a quick learner, so it's not surprising he soon realized that unlike China, the supply of wine (Chilean and others) in the U.S. exceeded the demand. Consequently, growth in the U.S. would be an uphill battle. The mandatory wholesaler tier has become more and more difficult to deal with, as in, "take on another wine brand, are you kidding?"

But Peter knew that despite the hurdles, he had some key brand equities and assets. For one thing, Don Mateo is a memorable brand name for a Chilean wine, and the brand symbol is both interesting and notable to consumers.

As you can see, the symbol/logo for Don Mateo is the Moai ("mo-eye"). These Moai are the monolithic statues of Easter Island, off the coast of Chile. According to the Don Mateo website, "they reflect our commitment to discovery, craftsmanship and passion. These three elements have been the guiding principles for Don Mateo wines from Chile." Might even stand for the three partners behind the venture. You never know.

If you asked the brand owners what the single most important asset of their wines is, their answer would most likely be "the wine." Trust me, these are outstanding wines. But in case you don't believe it, think about the medals they won at the WSWA: three silver and a double gold.

Here's the irony. Despite the entrepreneurial approach, despite their marketing and branding, and despite the high quality and good value, you'd think wholesalers would be beating a path to Don Mateo's door. Instead, getting wholesalers to take on the line has been slow and difficult. Such is the state of the **Booze Business**, due to the plethora of brands on the market.

But hey, the Moai on Easter Island have stood the test of time, so why shouldn't Don Mateo Wines?

Booze to Broadway to Booze Again

Wine and Spirits Daily and *Shanken Daily News* have each published stories on Hiro Sake and its co-founder Carlos Arana. In fact, there's been quite a bit of press about them.

Since I've known Carlos for most of my **Booze Business** days, I thought I would chime in.

At Seagram, Carlos and I suffered through the foibles of our boss and managed to survive the adventures of Patron in the early days. Carlos went on to run the Asia-Pacific whisk(e)y business.

Next came an 8-year stint with the Beckmann family; Carlos ran the tequila business with impressive results, and literally put Jose Cuervo on the global map. He managed to double sales and triple profits, and increased market share by five percentage points. Not too shabby.

A brief tour of duty as President of the Arnell Group was enough to convince him that doing your own thing is far more rewarding than working in a corporate setting.

Enter Broadway and Hiro Sake.

Carlos, for as long as I've known him, has wanted to be a producer, and already has a string of credits. He was co-producer for *La Cage aux Folles* revival (won a Tony); co-producer of *The Scottsboro Boys*; "above the title" producer credit for *On a Clear Day* and *The King's Speech*. He also owns the Latin America rights to *The Boy From Oz*, which he opened in Lima and expects to take on tour in the future. Since I'm a wannabe playwright learning about the theater business, all I can say is: this is most impressive for someone who's been at it for a short period of time.

While turning on lights on Broadway, Carlos and his partners launched Hiro Sake, a premium product brewed in Niigata, the prime sake-producing region of Japan. There is a Hiro Red (Junmai) and a Hiro Blue (Junmai Ginjo). What's particularly interesting to me is how they are marketing Hiro, an easily pronounced brand to call for by name. In addition, Hiro has all the tradition and heritage of sake, but appropriate as a cocktail as well. In fact, their focus is on both Asian and mainstream accounts.

I asked Carlos about the common denominator for Broadway ventures and launching a new booze product. He told me, "They have a lot in common...they each require unique ideas and development with innovation and passion."

Let's not forget sponsorship opportunities. For example, Hiro Sake has welcomed the debut of Japanese superstar Ryoko Yonekura as Roxy Hart in *Chicago*. The signature drink will be the funny, honey Hiro.

Sounds like they're on a roll.

*   *   *

Update:

As of 2015, Hiro Sake was awarded "Best Of Nation" by San Francisco International Wine Competition. On the Broadway front, Carlos has won two additional Tony's this past season.

*   *   *

Diströya: A Unique New Spiced Spirit

Diströya Spirits, Inc. is focused on building a trilogy of unique spirit flavors, each with its own story. First up: "The Dragon's Share," based on a mythological story about a spiced spirit created by the Viking King Magnus.

An article in *Epicurious* had this to say: "The Vikings might have bludgeoned you on the head with a club, but Diströya, a Viking-based 70-proof spirit, takes a rather more mellow approach when it assaults your senses."

I met the owner of Diströya Spirits a few years ago. He was (and still is) a reader and follower of my blog, and contacted me for some advice about the product he planned to launch. I get this type of call and email often, but this time it felt different. Scott Raynor, the owner, is an impressive guy. He's a musician (when he has time to work on that craft), an ex-bartender, and among the most tenacious and innovative **Booze Business** entrepreneurs I've met.

According to Scott, Diströya has less sugar and a lot more mystery than other liqueurs and shooters. "There's blood orange on the nose and entry, rounded out with vanilla, almond, and cinnamon in the middle, finishing with the crispness of ginger and citrus," he explains. "It's lighter than a lot of liqueurs, and not cloying."

While he describes his product as a liqueur, its official TTB classification, such a booze product by any other name is still a shooter. In fact, he cites his competitive set as Jägermeister, Fireball, and Kraken, among others. But Scott is savvy enough not to put his fledgling brand in a box, and reports that bartenders are using it in mojitos, as a Ginger Viking (a Moscow Mule), and in other cocktails. It sells for $19.99 for a 750ML.

I'm well past the shooter stage, and have a limited repertoire of cocktail preferences, so I enjoy it on the rocks. It's pleasant tasting, smooth, and makes me want to plunder and pillage. It's all that Scott says it is.

Despite the absence of meaningful resources, Scott's contagious enthusiasm, industry knowledge (self-taught), and likeability has attracted an all-star team of spirits industry mavens in sales and marketing. Add to that some outstanding designers and illustrators.
On a shoestring budget, he's managed to do what the big spirits boys cannot—form a team, launch a product, and build a brand. And he's doing it the hard way.

*   *   *

Update:

As of this writing, Diströya is in half a dozen markets (Colorado, Minnesota, Maryland, Washington D.C., New Jersey, New Hampshire, and Maine) and they have a football promotion going with Buffalo Wild Wings in Minnesota. While financial resources are still an issue, the brand is showing some progress.

*　　*　　*

Casa Dragones: Tequila with a Pedigree,

When passion and expertise meet, extraordinary tequila emerges.

Bob Pittman, a tequila aficionado, and Bertha González Nieves, a certified tequila expert and the first woman to be named Maestra Tequilera by the Academia Mexicana de Catadores de Tequila, founded Casa Dragones in 2008. At $275 per bottle, it is both exceptional and aspirational.

As the story goes, Bob Pittman (founder of MTV, CEO of Clear Channel) has spent many summers in San Miguel de Allende, where he has a home; and over the years, he became a true tequila lover. In 2007, Bob and Bertha met at a party and talked about their mutual passion for tequila. Bob shared his dream of creating one, and Bertha told him that she always wanted to become an entrepreneur. Together, they set on a quest to deliver a true sipping tequila—smooth enough to sip, with no "wince factor." A short time later, the two founded Casa Dragones.

I don't know Bob Pittman, but I do know Bertha González very well. She and I worked together when she was the Commercial Director, North America for Jose Cuervo International (JCI), and I was a consultant/advisor to the company. Actually, Bertha had a number of positions at JCI, under the leadership of Carlos Arana; including business development, new products, and brand management. In short, she knows tequila, and how to run a tequila enterprise.

While at JCI, I marveled at Bertha's ability to balance the whims of the Beckmann family (owners of Cuervo) and the arrogance of Diageo (distributors at the time). Clearly Bertha's wit, intellect, and charm came in handy.

Here's an example: a few years ago, when asked in an interview whether anyone ever mixed anything with Casa Dragones, Bertha's reply was, "not in front of me."

I guess the first thing everyone notices about the original Casa Dragones tequila is the price tag. If you're a particular type of spirits consumer, it's worth it. It's a 100% Blue Agave Joven Tequila, crafted in small batches. Joven tequila is a rare blend of silver tequila and extra-aged tequila. It's a style rarely used, and it took both Bertha and a master distiller, coaxed out of retirement, over a year to perfect the blend.

It's tequila to be sipped and savored and never, ever mixed. Trust me—it's not like any other tequila you've ever tasted. But don't take my word for it; *Wine Enthusiast* gave it a 96, and here is what Tequila.net had to say about it:

"From the soil to the Agave plant to the craftsmanship to the bottle—this is not tequila to use in a margarita or even as a shot." Like the lady said, sip it.

If you must drink your tequila in a cocktail, they have recently introduced Casa Dragones Blanco, 100% Blue Agave silver tequila, designed to be served on the rocks or in signature craft cocktails developed by leading bar chefs and mixologists. Cocktails like San Miguel, Pink Panther, and my favorite, Michelada Primaverde, are described on the website as follows:

James Beard Award Winning Mixologist and Owner of New York City's P.D.T (Please Don't Tell), Jim Meehan has created the Michelada Primaverde exclusively with Tequila Casa Dragones Blanco. A mixture of dry vermouth and tomatillo juice is complemented perfectly by a splash of Victoria beer and a spicy, salted rim for a refreshing, summer cocktail.

The Blanco sells for $75 for a 750 ML. Feel better now?

As to the heritage, the elite cavalry that helped spark the Mexican independence movement inspires the name. La Casa Dragones—the original 17th century stables still standing on a street in San Miguel de Allende—is the spiritual home to the tequila.

What makes Casa Dragones especially unique is that it's thoroughly Mexican. It is a product that comes from the lowlands and the rich soil of the Trans-Mexican volcanic belt; a formula based on the merging of the traditional art of tequila making with an innovative process; a product designed for a consumer who is looking for quality and authenticity. It's the real deal.

It's also about Bertha González Nieves and her passion for tequila and innovation. Add her to the list of **Booze Business** Shakers and Stirrers—the new breed of alcohol industry entrepreneurs.

Just don't let her catch you drinking the Joven product with a mixer.

*   *   *

While there are many wannabe spirits industry tycoons out there who are sadly heading toward failure, it's comforting to know that there are those with the tenacity and patience to make it. The people you've just met are not dreamers; they are hardworking men and women who understand the obstacles, and are working their way through the alcohol industry jungle.

To me, they are the future of the Booze Business. I feel very encouraged when I meet and spend time with them. So I'll keep looking.

*   *   *

At a social gathering, Jack Summers of Sorel and Marco Destefanis and Carlos Arana of Hiro Sake got into a conversation about how hard they worked at building their brands. Jack pointed out that his day starts with tons of paperwork, followed by retail and bar calls all day; while the evenings (when he's not at an event) are spent in his bottling facility, then back to paperwork. Marco asked, "When do you sleep?" To which Jack replied, "I'll sleep when I'm dead."

*   *   *

So...what does it take to succeed?

The most common definition of an entrepreneur is "a person who organizes and operates a business or businesses, taking on greater than normal financial risks in order to do so." The people you've met in this chapter have more than just *that* going for them. They have vision, patience, and determination. They surround themselves with smart and dedicated people who want them to succeed, and then they rely on their network.

Above all, they have the wisdom to understand that no matter how hard they work to produce their product, unless they reach the people at the other end of the bottle, they won't win. "Make it and they will buy" just doesn't work.

The startups I admire and would like to help the most are in it for the long haul. I once asked someone who had approached me about consulting with him, "What's your exit strategy?" He said, "There is none." I couldn't wait to get started.

6. Industry Legends—Thinking outside the bottle

In many respects, the startups in the last chapter aspire to be the entrepreneurs and industry leaders in this chapter. The common denominators of the people I'll focus on are innovation, tenacity, and outside-the-box thinking.

Without exception, they are not typical corporate **Booze Business** types. They are free thinkers and risk takers. They are natural born marketers who understand people and what motivates them.

Based on past and current experience, I know it's rare to find senior, or even top management, with these traits in corporations. The corporate system either punishes failure (so why take the chance?) or lacks the patience to see an innovation come to fruition. That's why the large liquor companies are more inclined to buy brands rather than invent them.

The other factor is following the money. Not only does survival depend on making the plan, but also bonuses are not paid for risk taking. If you're running a large spirits company, which would you rather emphasize: a hand truck of a new product, or a pallet of your leading brand? I'm not saying it's impossible to do both, but that doesn't seem to apply in most liquor (or beer or wine) companies.

*   *   *

Michel Roux: The Man Who Put Absolut on the Map

The Seagram Gulfstream took off from Stockholm's Arlanda airport with a full load of executives; and all of them had the satisfaction of knowing the global distribution rights to Absolut were signed, sealed, and delivered. Every one of the 14 plane seats was taken, and there was no place to hide. And every one of the 14 had 5 or 6 ideas each about marketing, and how best to grow the brand further. After all, we were taking over the brand from the legendary Michel Roux, who grew the brand with a series of inventive and effective marketing actions, not least of which was the advertising campaign.

While gaining the brand elated us, we were also mindful of the daunting task ahead. Especially the marketing guy—me.

Michel Roux was indeed a hard act to follow. He was President and CEO of Carillon Importers, a division of a larger corporation that ultimately became Diageo. Yet Michel ran the brand entrepreneurially, with vision and resources to take the fledgling brand to renowned marketing level, changing a category forever.

There is a great story about Michel's brand champion efforts that I asked him to confirm. I wasn't sure if it was true, or a **Booze Business** myth.

It seems he was in the Detroit airport waiting to depart, when he noticed a man wearing an Absolut t-shirt. Alarm bells went off in his head for two reasons: First, there were no Absolut t-shirts because he didn't want them, so clearly it was counterfeit. Second and most important, the man in question (according to Michel) must have weighed over 350 pounds, and despite the triple XL size, it was a very snug fit.

Clearly bothered by his brand being portrayed in such a manner, Roux stopped the man, told him he was looking for that particular t-shirt, and offered him $100 to buy it. The man accepted the generous offer. They went to a souvenir store and bought him another t-shirt as a replacement.

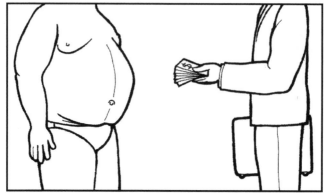

"ON BEHALF OF THE XYZ SWIMSUIT COMPANY, HERE'S $1,000 TO BUY ANOTHER BATHING SUIT."

The man left happy with this transaction, and the Absolut t-shirt was promptly tossed in the trash.

True story.

In my opinion, the Absolut brand has gone through four periods in its development. The first era was with M. Roux and Carillon Importers. Next came the Seagram years and further, albeit different, growth. The third period was one in which the brand began to languish, despite the efforts of some capable people. Today, the ownership of the brand is in the hands of Pernod-Ricard, with the difficult task of once again polishing its luster.

Find a hole and fill it

My blog has given me the opportunity to reconnect with old friends and to make new ones, like David van de Velde, whose business motto is the headline for this posting.

In addition to being a smart and affable fellow, David is an interesting entrepreneur who created Ketel One and Van Gogh Vodkas. In that regard, he changed the spirits industry.

Let's start with the motto. In an age of me-tooism, finding a hole and filling it speaks volumes about brand development strategies.

Not long after Seagram got Absolut Vodka, I kept hearing about this new brand, Ketel One; it was unique in its packaging, name, underlying concept, and had one other "outrageous" factor... a price at a significant premium to the category.

In addition, Ketel One concentrated on bartenders and servers, used videos and events to tell their story, and even used special olives for a martini. Everywhere I went at the time, all I heard about was how we needed to learn from the Ketel One people.

Many people think that Grey Goose created the ultra premium vodka market; when in fact, by the time Grey Goose came along, Ketel was already doing 200,000 cases.

David's understanding of consumers is very impressive. He describes the target customer for high-end vodkas at that time as someone who wears Armani suits without pockets. Someone who walks into a bar holding car keys with a Mercedes or BMW logo, an expensive cell phone, and a wallet chock-full of goodies. No pockets. The question he asked himself is—would this person drink anything but a top shelf brand?

After Ketel One, he created Van Gogh vodka, and brought the flavored category to new levels.

King Cocktail's New Venture

Dale DeGoff is a **Booze Business** entrepreneur and somewhat of a renaissance man. His latest endeavor moved him from behind the bar into the realm of a manufacturer. He's been credited as the inventor of the Cosmo; and more importantly, he's a really nice guy.

I first met Dale back in the day, when he was tending bar at some great places, most notably the Rainbow Room. From that point on, he was at the forefront of what's been described as the gourmet (or mixologist) approach toward cocktails, particularly the classics.

I suppose that's why he's known as King Cocktail, although I think of him as a **Booze Business** equivalent of Wolfgang Puck—a celebrity barman (but without an accent).

The man has a list of awards, including the James Beard Award for Wine & Spirits, and has written a number of books including *The Craft of the Cocktail*. He's a partner in a bar training program called Beverage Alcohol Resource (BAR, get it?) and he's the founding president of The Museum of the American Cocktail. He also tours the country with a one-man show called "ON THE TOWN! A Tribute to Bars, Speaks, & Legendary Saloons."

You'd think that would be enough to keep him busy, right? Wrong. Dale has recently launched his own brand of bitters called Dale DeGoff's Pimento Aromatic Bitters. It's designed to be very similar to Pimento Dram, an ingredient Dale often used, but is no longer available. He joined forces with Ted Breaux, of recent Absinthe fame, to produce it.

I think that before I go any further, we should talk about bitters and their use in cocktails. If you're a booze maven, you probably know this already, but indulge me anyhow.

Bitters are an alcohol beverage (DeGoff's is 90-proof) flavored with a range of herbs and spices. Add a little bit of bitters to cocktails, and you won't believe how it enhances the flavor and taste.

Dale uses select botanicals and allspice, which is made from the pimento berry (not to be confused with the little red things stuffed in olives).

So Mr. DeGoff jumps over the bar and joins the ranks of other bar personalities and companies making commercial bitters, including Gary Regan (Regan's Orange Bitters No. 6), Angostura, Peychaud, and others.

Welcome to the producer's side of the bar, Dale.

The Inventor

Maurice Kanbar is among a select group of entrepreneurs who have changed the spirits industry. And he's still at it.

Like my earlier posting about David van de Velde, Maurice is another visionary businessman who has spent a lifetime finding a hole and filling it. Maurice has been inventing, designing, and developing a host of products ranging from films, to surgical instruments, to things that might make you say, "why didn't I think of that?") The man has thirty patents and products to his credit.

I first met Maurice in the early days of Skyy Spirits, when I was sent on a fool's errand to see if he would be willing to chat about an acquisition. This was in the late 1990s, and the brand was just starting its ascendency. We were feeling the effects of its growth, and one of the geniuses in Sweden thought we might be able to "buy him out." After just a few minutes of chatting, Maurice asked the key question—why sell while the brand is still growing? Duh. Sure got my respect.

What I really admire about him is his judgment and intuition, balanced by the tenacity of an inventive mind.

Examples:

He complains to a doctor friend that he gets headaches and a hangover from Cognac. His friend explains about congeners, and tells him to drink vodka. The next thing he knows, he's studying the world of spirits, making advancements to the distillation and filtering systems, and creating Skyy Vodka.

At the time, no one in the food or beverage industries used blue for packaging; don't ask me why. I once got my butt chewed for presenting a new product in blue packaging. Maurice didn't let this narrow in-the-box thinking confine him. I don't know for sure, but I suppose he was thinking Skyy = blue. Another duh.

When his brand started growing, he was smart enough to surround himself with people who knew the business.

He's an interesting guy, to say the least.

His newest effort is Blue Angel Vodka; he says it's based on advancement in distillation that produces an ultra smooth product. But the really cool part about it, in my opinion, is that the inventor has further increased his marketing skills. First, his signature drink is the Blue Angel Martini (BAM, as he calls it) made with blue curacao. I also like his tongue-in-cheek slogan: "the world's second best vodka; we're still looking for the best."

On second thought, maybe he should stick to inventing.

The Bartender's Bartender

Ray Foley is many things—a bartender, writer and publisher, drink creator, storyteller, entrepreneur, and ex-marine—but don't ever refer to him as a mixologist.

Anyone who has been in the **Booze Business** knows that it's the men and women behind the bar who build brands, invent drinks, and provide the backbone of the business. Let's face it, it wasn't a suit that created the Cosmo or any other top drink—it was a barkeep.

I first met Ray at Seagram; everyone talked about the Fuzzy Navel, and credited him with the idea. More importantly, of all the publishers and sales reps who called on me, he was among the very few who understood the business and the important on-premise trade.

In the intervening years, he has continued to reach over 100,000 bartenders in *Bartender Magazine* and hundreds of thousands on Bartender. com. He and his wife Jaclyn have been running the magazine for over 30 years. Together, they've created the Bartender Hall of Fame, and run a foundation to provide scholarships for bartenders and their children.

Ray has written dozens of books, including *Bartending for Dummies*; the perfect title for an outspoken, take-no-prisoners ex-Marine who hates BS and some of the changes he's seen in the bartending profession. But I'll let you in on a secret: deep down, he's a kind and gentle man who speaks his mind, but carries no malice.

Take the term "mixologist." Here's a quote I found from him in New Jersey Magazine: "A mixologist is a person who really doesn't know how to tend bar but has the money to get a PR agent." Ray told me pretty much the same thing when I interviewed him for this posting, but went on to add that while he has no argument with the phrase, and much respect for the serious mixologists, it's those who are all ego and no skill that get his Irish up. If you call yourself "The Bar Guru" or "Mr. Mojito," stay out of his way.

Ray comes from the school of thought that a good bartender is partly a person who serves drinks, and mainly a person who does so with personality and good customer service.

When I was running new products at Seagram and we needed a signature drink to make the brand take hold, I learned two important things from Ray. The first was to let the drink idea come organically from behind the bar, from the bartender or (forgive me, Ray) the mixologist. In other words, let the professionals do it, and keep the marketing suits out of the kitchen.

The second thing was, in order for a drink recipe to take hold, keep it simple. According to Ray, "Creating a drink with avocado juice and lemongrass doesn't impress me...how many bars have those ingredients?"

Of all the thousands of people who read **Booze Business**, I generally think about Ray when I do a posting. He never hesitates to let me know what he thinks, and generally the emails from Ray have been helpful and positive.

Except when I use the dreaded 'mixologist' word.

Tom Jago: The man who changed the face of spirits

He is the creator of Baileys Irish Cream, and the creative force behind Johnnie Walker Blue and many other brands.

I first met Tom Jago in the early 1990s when he was part of James Espey's scotch and cognac team at Seagram. My immediate reaction was: here is a man who is gifted in product development and marketing. He's also affable and enjoyable to be around. I'm not sure he's really British.

Over the years, Tom taught me a great deal about the spirits business, and above all, about how to choose and enjoy good Claret (Bordeaux).

Together with Dr. Espey and Mr. Peter Fleck, he is now a principal in the Last Drop Distillers Ltd.

Here's how their website describes Tom:

From a village school in the remote countryside, via a scholarship to Oxford and service in the Royal Navy during WWII, Tom Jago found his niche in the wine and spirits trade. He led the team that developed new ideas on old themes, like Croft Original Pale Cream Sherry and Le Piat D'Or brands, which revolutionised British drinking habits forever. He cooperated with the "gang of three" in the invention of Bailey's Irish Cream and Malibu.

Additionally, Tom was instrumental (as in, the driving force) in creating such brands as Johnnie Walker Blue Label, Hennessy, Chivas Regal 18 Year Old, Martell, The Classic Malts, and many others.

If that's not enough, while at Seagram, Tom helped with the creation of Imperial Blue and Royal Stag, now an important part of Pernod India.

I've spent time talking and emailing with Tom, and have gotten his thoughts on the industry.

After the war, Tom "slipped accidentally into advertising." He applied for a job as a photographer, but was mistaken for someone else, and got a job as a copywriter. He later became an account director at an ad agency that ultimately became Ogilvy & Mather. Among his clients was Gilbeys, a small company that hired him. Through mergers and acquisitions, Gilbeys became IDV and finally Diageo.

Next came four years at Moet-Hennessy, followed by United Distillers (with James Espey), and later Seagram.

The area of focus throughout Tom's career was innovation and new products. As Tom puts it, "I was not very good at being a marketing director (at Gilbeys), so they gave me a small budget, an office and secretary, and said, 'try to think of some new drinks we might profitably sell.'" Based on the brands he has developed over the years, I'd say he has come up with quite a few.

Tom's focus over the years has been based on simple and straightforward guiding principles.

First, "Make the drink agreeable to the palate, the eye, and the nose. Baileys and Malibu are good examples of this."

A second principle was to develop products that would inherently persuade drinkers there is virtue in drinking them, and in learning to appreciate their quality. Interestingly, Tom applied these same motivations of palate, eyes, and nose to whisky, cognac, and even tequila.

Above all, Tom has a powerful way of looking at the acceptance and growth of a brand—with patience. "It is clear to me that the motivation to drink alcohol is very deeply buried in the human subconscious... therefore, attempts to market distilled spirits must be subtle too," Tom told me. "A spirits brand is bound to be slow growing, so promotions must be long, steady, and consistent."

In my experience, new products and brands often fail because the companies behind them, particularly the global ones, lack the fortitude to see them through to fruition. That's why the successes in the U.S. (e.g. Grey Goose and Patron) have come from entrepreneurs.

Another worthwhile notion from Tom is not to let drinker research get in the way. "It is of course useful, but in the specific case of alcohol drinks, not to be relied on, given the essential illogical responses of people to alcohol," says Tom. "No one will tell you the truth about their feelings regarding drinks—mainly because they don't know what they are themselves."

Despite the drink inventions that favor light, sweet, and palatable drinks, Tom is an unabashed devotee of Malts.

"These are, I must confess, my favorite of all the alcoholic drinks... I admire them partly because of their enormous variety of nose and taste (cognac, no matter how fine, all tastes much the same—compared with the vast difference between a malt from Islay and one from the Spey). Much of their appeal, of course, lies in their relative rarity—the amateur can 'discover' them for himself, so he feels that he owns a part of the brand. It is interesting that when a malt gets as big (in volume sales) as, for instance, Glenfiddich or the Glenlivet, people stop thinking of it as a malt, and rather as just another Scotch brand."

Tom's focus on whisky over the years has been extraordinary. Johnnie Walker Blue Label was created in 1987 to reassert the perceived value of the Johnnie Walker brand in Asia, where grey market discounting had damaged it. He also developed Classic Malts, a collection of outstanding products from individual malt distilleries, which later became brands.

At his current venture, Last Drop Distillers Ltd., Tom and his partners are using 70 single malts in their blend. Some are from distilleries long since closed. It's truly an amazing venture, and you might want to look it up.

Throughout his career, Tom helped to define and advance product quality. While at Hennessy, for example, he learned about the sophisticated use of oak in spirit maturation. No one in the scotch business knew about this at the time, and one can only imagine the battles that ensued between this young upstart and the tough, crusty old timers who ran the whisky production.

Perhaps because of these battles, or just his plain good common sense, Tom taught me to be wary of production managers.

"A word of caution concerning those splendid fellows…Don't let them ruin a great luxury brand by economy measures unrelated to the essential perceived value of the pack; I have seen a production man try to save less than a penny by spoiling the closure of Johnnie Walker Blue Label—this on a brand that sells for £100."

Larry Ruvo: A True Renaissance Man

Distributor, Marketer, Philanthropist, and all-around Mensch

Larry Ruvo, who runs Southern Wine and Spirits of Nevada, is in my opinion the most extraordinary person in the Booze Business. He's a distributor, an outstanding marketer, and a philanthropist. If you Google "Renaissance man," it might as well show his picture—*a person with many talents or areas of knowledge.*

He started in his family-owned Las Vegas restaurant, worked as the GM of the LA Playboy Club, ran the Sahara and The Frontier, opened

Caesar's Palace, and joined with Steve Wynn in starting a wine and spirits distribution company. That company became SWS of Nevada. So most people think of him as Mr. Las Vegas.

But that doesn't begin to describe the kind of man he is.

The myth that suppliers (manufacturers) would have you believe is that distributors/wholesalers are a necessary burden. The law mandates them, they'll tell you, but all they really do is move your box from their warehouse to the trade. Let me tell you, folks—in Larry's case, nothing could be further from the truth.

When I was running U.S. marketing at Seagram, the senior executives made biannual market visits. On these tours were the top brass, the sales guys, the finance people, and the marketing guy—me. Truth be told, I never really learned anything on these Tunnel of Love tours that I didn't already know. Except for the visits to Las Vegas, when I had the opportunity to talk with Larry about his brand building and marketing ideas. He was willing— no, make that eager—to talk about what motivates consumers, bar owners, and bartenders, and the best ways to get a brand featured and showcased. I learned a ton from Larry Ruvo.

I can't remember how many Seagram sales incentive and achievement trips my wife and I took when I was with the company. But whenever Larry and his wife Camille (whose birth date I share) were on the trip, we knew it would be special. Whether it was a dinner in the kitchen of an amazing restaurant in Bilbao, the best shopping in Hong Kong, or lunch on the Amalfie coast, Larry knew the places to go, what to see, where to eat, how to make it more enjoyable. And he delighted in sharing these things.

Larry does things with passion and total commitment, so when he turned his attention to fighting brain-damaging illnesses, it wasn't surprising that wonderful things began to happen.

He is the founder and chairman of Keep Memory Alive, a foundation that built and supports the Lou Ruvo Center for Brain Health in Las Vegas (also known as the Cleveland Clinic Lou Ruvo Center for Brain Health). Its mission is to treat patients with brain disorders such as Alzheimer's, Huntington's, Parkinson's, ALS, and Multiple Sclerosis. Since its inception, the foundation has raised over $235 million and treated over 23,000 patients (as of this writing).

It all started in 1995, on the one-year anniversary of his father Lou's death from Alzheimer's. Larry gathered 35 friends for a private dinner at Spago to "laugh, reminisce, and tell Lou Ruvo stories." As the night wore on, it turned from an event to honor his father to a call for action to defeat the disease that took his father's life. They raised $35,000 and the foundation was born.

The biggest challenge was being taken seriously, since Las Vegas is not top of mind for world-class health and wellness facilities. But in the last 10 years, thanks to Larry's marketing, packaging, and brand building skills, the city has become known for those very things.

To meet the challenge, Larry created the Power of Love Gala in Las Vegas and raised money to fund his plans. He convinced Frank Gehry to design the building, and it's truly amazing. Next, he signed a deal with Cleveland Clinic to operate it; but he also needed a superstar to run it. So he turned to Cleveland Clinic and said, "I'm giving you Yankee Stadium... I want Babe Ruth." What he got was Dr. Jeffrey L. Cummings, a world-renowned leader in research and treatment of brain disorders.
That's what happens, my friends, when you mix determination, passion, and marketing skills.

His foundation, Keep Memory Alive, and the Cleveland Clinic Lou Ruvo Center for Brain Health, holds an annual fundraising event in Las Vegas. It's called The Power of Love, and in the past it has honored Muhammad Ali, Quincy Jones, Sir Michael Caine, and many others.
When Larry Ruvo sets his sights on something, great things happen.

Gary (gaz) Regan: A Man For All Seasons

Bartender, innovator, author, publisher, educator, and more.

I first met gaz (he spells his name without capital letters) in the early 1990s when I was at Seagram. While I've always known him as Gary, the name "gaz" is his nickname, and became his nom de plume some time ago. Whatever he calls himself, he's a heck of a guy, and has made major contributions to the **Booze Business**.

Before I get into all that, here's a story I heard from gaz.

I heard it on his radio show (with Paul Pacult) in the late 90s. They invited me on, and we were discussing single malt scotches in general and The Glenlivet (a Seagram brand at the time) in particular.

To illustrate the nature of the category, gaz told a story about when he was bartending in the 1980s on South Street in NYC. It seems that a particular Scottish gentleman would come in for lunch everyday, order a hamburger, and asks for the "book." It was a guide to single malt scotches and differences in brands, regions, water, grain, and distillation styles. After work, the gentleman would meet with friends and colleagues and hold forth on the verities of various malts. While he sounded like an authority on the subject, the information he provided was less than 5 hours old.
To me, the story illustrated the nature of the single malt category, and the focus among those drinkers on discovery and what's in the bottle.

There are two other things I learned from gaz: the power of stories in the **Booze Business**, and the crucial role of the bartender.

Did I say he was a writer? I meant to say prolific writer. He has written a column for the San Francisco Chronicle for 14 years, publishes three newsletters a week, won two Best Cocktail Writer awards, and wrote more than a dozen books. He is also both a regular contributor to Liquor.com, and an advisory board member.

If you want to reach bartenders, gaz is the man to see. Two of his books, *gaz regan's Annual Manual for Bartenders* and *101 Best New Cocktails* are published annually, and reach a wide audience all over the world. Oh, and let's not forget *The Joy of Mixology* and *The Bartender's Bible.*

My favorite is *The Negroni: A gaz regan Notion*, the second edition of which was recently released. Not only has he made that drink famous, but he has also cleared up many of the myths surrounding its origin. All I'll tell you is that it was named for one Count Negroni, the broncobuster who first created the drink in the early years of the 20th century. It's a fun read.

Credited by many as one of the godfathers of the mixology movement, gaz is a bartender's bartender. In addition to books and bartending appearances (The Dead Rabbit in NYC), one of his newsletters is devoted to job opportunities around the world. Mention his name to any professional bartender, and their eyes will light up and a big smile will appear. Along with other famed bartenders like Dale DeGroff, gaz has been a judge at Diageo's World Class Bartending Competition.

In fact, companies like Diageo and Pernod Ricard have been smart enough to avail themselves of his services. I think it's because he has his fingers on the pulse of the bar trade—consumer and bartender. That is, of course, when his finger is not stirring one of his world-class Negronis.

gaz came up with the Just One Shift idea to help raise money for a charity called Wine to Water, which has been bringing potable water to thousands of people all over the world since 2004. Doc Hendley, a bartender from North Carolina, founded Wine to Water.

Each year, gaz organizes and promotes a campaign for bartenders to contribute the tips from "just one shift," and 100% of what they raise brings clean water to needy people worldwide.

Cocktails in the Country, a bartender event, ran for seven years from 2001 until 2007. gaz decided to bring it back in 2015, and from what bartenders have told me, that's great news. Cocktails in the Country is a Master Class focusing on the importance of service in the hospitality business.

Held in Cornwall on Hudson NY, the two-day bartender workshop covers a wide range of issues for the trade. It even culminates in a special bartending certification.

*   *   *

The people you've met in this chapter are only a small sampling of those who have changed the spirits business; as suppliers, new product inventers, distributors, and bartender/mixologists. These are all people who love the **Booze Business**, and possess the pioneering spirit and self-confidence to take risks.

7. Celebrity Booze—Here comes the 'A' list

It never ceases to amaze me how many celebrities and people of questionable fame try to enter the Booze Business, either by licensing their name or providing a paid endorsement. I suppose they believe that it's easy money, passive income, a way to leverage their success, or who knows what else. Almost all of them fail. Yet every year, celebrity booze products enter the market.

*   *   *

Star Power Booze

Celebrity endorsed or owned liquor products, with a few notable exceptions, nearly always fail. So why do these products keep coming out?

First I'll mention those that seem to have made it.

Top of the list is P. Diddy and Cîroc. The brand started without him; but with him, it has gone through the roof. He has a following, and with an interest in the brand, his marketing has paid off. Next up is Sobieski, with a Bruce Willis connection. Willis licensed his image, for which he received shares in the parent company. Is it Willis or the attractive price point that made the brand strong? Dan Aykroyd and Crystal Head seem to be doing well.

Then there is Bethenny Frankel and Skinny Girl. Although in recent years, the allure of this brand has been slipping.

But the list of failed booze products with celebrity ownership/tie-in is large. Donald Trump, Ludacris, Roberto Cavalli, Willie Nelson, Danny DeVito, Marilyn Manson, Justin Timberlake, Frida Kahlo—just to name a few.

In the never-made-it-off-the-ground category:

Remember Psy and Gangnam Style stuff? A Russian company called Woobo International had planned to use the phrase "Oppah, Gangnam Style" to promote a brand of vodka in Russia. Huh?

How about this one? The *LA Times* and the *NY Post* reported in 2013 that Shaquille O'Neal planned to start his own vodka. The booze was named "Luv Shaq." The bottles would be emblazoned with images of a winged O'Neal, and produced in partnership with Devotion Vodka. "Luv Shaq?" Really?

Undoubtedly, there will be more to come. And failures will abound. When will the stars learn that in the **Booze Business**, it's as much about the product as it is about them? Think about the uniqueness of Cîroc or the Skinny Girl proposition or the packaging of Crystal Head.

My advice—if you want to go into the **Booze Business**, your name alone is not enough.

*　　　*　　　*

A closer look at celebrity booze

We can understand why celebrities would license their names. Usually, for very little effort, there is the possibility of handsome returns and occasionally guaranteed minimum royalties. For the licensor (supplier), there is the belief that "borrowed credentials" via a widely known and recognizable name presents the potential to break through the clutter, and might be a shortcut to success.

But the real judge is the consumer. For many, celebrity booze represents a frivolous effort and lacks authenticity. As consumers think more and more about what's in the bottle, a spirits or wine product needs more than a recognizable name.

Let's look at some of the successful ones more closely:

- Casamigos for George Clooney will succeed because of his commitment to the brand, his following, and his extremely positive public image. But just as important, if not more so, is that the product is excellent tequila, and his message to the consumer resonates—"Brought to You By Those Who Drink It." He's involved with the product, and is leveraging his fame among early adopters and opinion leaders.

- Cîroc is successful because of P. Diddy's following, involvement, and the uniqueness of the product and the flavors.

- Greg Norman Wine may have started with his name and fame, but the wine is considered first-rate, with a range of variants and value.

- Crystal Head Vodka by Dan Aykroyd has unique packaging, and he personally works at promoting it.

The common denominator is the willingness of the celebrity to get involved in the product and its promotion. Those who work it, succeed. Those who sit around waiting for a check, ultimately lose.

*　　*　　*

More Tequila Tales

The story of Jimmy Buffett, Seagram, and Tequila.

The caller was annoyed and had a threatening tone in his voice. He got right to the point, informing me that he was a business manager for Jimmy Buffett. He added quickly that we had infringed on trademark and other intellectual property rights; I can't recall the full extent of our alleged violations, but I was intrigued.

When I politely asked, "What the hell are you talking about?" he explained that Parrot Bay Rum by Captain Morgan—which had recently been introduced—infringed on their established use of the term Parrott Head, the commonly-used nickname for fans of Jimmy Buffett. (I remember thinking, "Is he nuts? How do you trademark the term *parrot*?")

I knew who Buffett was, and associated him with the song "Margaritaville," but I was far from a fan, much less an aficionado. I knew he had a strong and loyal following, but that was about it.

Instinct told me this gentleman had more on his mind than a lawsuit—so I pushed back.

"I don't know what you're talking about," I countered. "Two floors below there are offices chock-full of lawyers who spend their time dealing with real and frivolous issues, so I suggest you take your best shot and do what you need to do." There was silence, but I could hear him blink. "Now do you want to tell me why you're really calling?"

He went on to explain that Buffett's team would like to have private label tequila for their restaurants; and since we didn't have a decent brand (that hurt), would we be interested in producing one for them?

My response was, "Listen... private label tequila is not a good idea. You'll make a nickel and we'll make a dime. It won't be anything more than a well brand (a low-end brand kept under the bar for drinks not identified by a brand name). Tell you what—let's talk about licensing Jimmy Buffett's name for a tequila."

The glee in his voice told me that I had just been played, but no matter; we needed a tequila brand, and this might just be the ticket.

He informed me they would prefer to use the name "Margaritaville," but the look and feel would be totally Buffett.

It didn't take long to consider—particularly since a friend and wholesaler, one of the best and smartest in the business, recommended him to us. The deal was done, so far as I was concerned. Getting approval from management (not the owners, this time) was another matter. It took a while.

Buffett's man lived up to his end of the deal—wouldn't you, if you got a hefty royalty off the top? As for me, I became much more than just a fan of Buffett, his music (I made my kids so crazy by playing it, they refused to ride in the car with me), his business, and of course, his live shows.

The biggest issue in the development was capturing the essence of the Jimmy Buffett brand. To my surprise, Jimmy himself appeared at the office, and let us know that he was there to help with the back label copy. In twenty minutes, he produced the most incredible story—that was totally Buffett. He is an amazing guy, superlative performer, accomplished author, and a decent, down-to-earth person.

In the few years that Seagram distributed the brand, before the lights went out, it went from 5,000 to 50,000 cases. Afterward it continued to grow, but was bounced from company to company, without (in my opinion) any significant focus or direction.

There is a happy ending, however. Margaritaville is now part of the Sazerac Company, and in good hands, selling around 300,000 9-litre cases. In addition to the original tequila brands, they also have rum and prepared cocktails, including a skinny margarita mix.

Reminds me of his song, "Changes in Latitude, Changes in Attitude"—nothing remains quite the same.

NOTHING REMAINS QUITE THE SAME.

Casamigos Tequila Joins Sidney Frank Importing Company

Sidney Frank Importing Co. (known for Jägermeister and the creation of Grey Goose Vodka) has been named the exclusive importer of Casamigos Tequila.

Will this celebrity spirit succeed? I think so.

First of all, Sidney Frank Importing Co. (SFIC) is a significant player in the **Booze Business**; their infrastructure, sales and marketing people, and distributor network is top of the game. The gents running it are seasoned veterans and brand builders—so put a double check mark next to the trade-marketing box.

But the consumer is the ultimate judge and most critical component of brand success. Casamigos will need to challenge some pretty tough, top shelf competition: including Patron, Don Julio, and strong newcomer Avión. And let's not forget Mr. Diddy's new tequila venture, DeLeón Tequila.

Some of the key elements of successful new entries? Awareness, curiosity, and a willingness to try.

Imagine this: you're in a bar with friends, and someone says, "Hey, let's have some tequila." Someone else says, "Great idea, I'd like to try that new George Clooney tequila." Another says, "Oh I love George Clooney—great actor, and he seems like a decent, down to earth guy. Let's buy a round."

So... thanks to SFIC's clout, the bar or restaurant will have Casamigos in stock. And thanks to George Clooney, the consumer is very likely to try the brand.

In the brand building equation, if there is uniqueness and relevance (Clooney and tequila), awareness will very often lead to trial.

The most important elements in the equation, however, are brand adoption and loyalty (sustained usage). If the quality of the tequila is high, and Mr. Clooney helps in the promotion, I think the brand will be around for the long run. I also believe it will be a success because Steve Bellini runs Business Intelligence and Trade Development at SFIC. Steve is my former and last boss at Seagram, and arguably the best sales person in the business.

So move over, Diddy—there may be a new player in town.

*   *   *

Update:

As of this writing, the Jägermeister Company acquired SFIC and Casamigos is marketing and selling the brand by themselves.

*   *   *

Chivas Regal and Hollywood Friends

The ultimate celebrity story—Lauren Bacall, Gregory Peck, and Frank Sinatra.

When Seagram was alive and well, they hosted many sponsored events, particularly when Universal-MCA was in the picture. It was not unusual, therefore, for the company to be front and center, underwriting the event (or parts of it) in exchange for publicity and press. In addition to the "Step and Repeat" backdrop, the sponsoring brand received widespread exposure and linkage to celebrities.

Some events were strictly sponsorship (e.g. Crown Royal and the Rodeo) and many were charity events that a particular brand supported or even underwrote.

I'd like to tell you the story about one such charity event involving Lauren Bacall.

It was in the late 1990s, and the Design Industries Foundation Fighting Aids (DIFFA) and the Motion Picture & Television Fund (MPTF) organized the fundraising dinner. Since it was held at the Cipriani in lower Manhattan, it was way beyond a rubber chicken dinner. Chivas was the sponsor, and other Seagram spirits and wines were served.

Based on the cause and the Universal-MCA connection, the attendees were all "A-list." I remember stars of stage, screen, and the fashion world in attendance; including Lauren Bacall, Michael Douglas, Richard Gere, and Vera Wang, to name a few. It must have been a harrowing experience, organizing and executing the event and photo shoots. But the Seagram corporate PR people, led by Karin Timpone, had it under control.

I wish I could find the photo that included yours truly, Lauren Bacall, and a number of others (whose names escape me). But trust me when I say it was a hoot to pose with the legendary Ms. Bacall, a Tony and Golden Globe winner and Oscar nominee. I'm guessing that she must have been in her late 70s at the time, and still extraordinarily classy and impressive. I'm rarely star struck, but come on—Bacall starred with (and was married to) Humphrey Bogart, and was in films with Kirk Douglas and Gary Cooper. She's an icon of theater and film.

The photo shoot ended. I thanked her for coming, for the opportunity to pose with her, and expressed gratitude on behalf of Chivas Regal. Her response was a courtly nod, and she also said, "I like Chivas Regal, can I get some sent to my home?" "Of course Ms. Bacall," I replied, and asked Karin to have someone arrange for a case of Chivas to be delivered to her.

I no sooner got the words out, when she added, "You know, my friend Gregory Peck also likes Chivas Regal, can you get a case to him in Palm Springs?" Gregory Peck? Holy cow; her co-star in the film *Designing Woman*, and one of my favorite actors. I couldn't get these words out fast enough—"Certainly… absolutely… we'll take care of it." She thanked me and the session was over.

I totally forgot about the incident. Sometime later in the spring of 1998, I received this letter from Gregory Peck:

Dear Arthur,

Our thanks for the beautiful gift of a case of Chivas Regal. I am a great admirer of this beverage.

Contrary to popular belief, our friend Frank Sinatra did not partake exclusively of Jack Daniel's. In his desert retreat, he sometimes joined me in a Chivas and Perrier, with perhaps a lemon twist, or a dash of bitters.

With appreciation and best regards,

(Signed)

Gregory Peck

The letter was dated May 26, 1998, and Frank Sinatra died on May 14, 1998—hence, the reference to Sinatra.

But I was puzzled. Did Lauren Bacall get her case of Chivas? I was assured that it had been delivered, but no acknowledgment was received. Oh well, that's show business. I didn't give it another thought.

That is, until a few months later.

I was having lunch with a good friend and principal of an ad agency. I told him the whole story, expressing my thrill at the Gregory Peck note, and surprise at the lack of response from Lauren Bacall. He laughed, and said that he had an interesting comparable experience to share.

It turns out that his agency had hired Bacall to be the voiceover for a cat food commercial. It was undoubtedly a 7-figure deal. After the day's shoot was done, she told a production assistant that she'd like to have a case of cat food sent to her home. The agency decided to send a case of each of the varieties, perhaps 3 or 4 cases of cat food.

"Did you hear back from her?" I asked.

"Nope, not a word... and here's the strange part... we found out she doesn't even own a cat."

But I bet she drank the Chivas Regal.

8. Vodka—From birth to old age

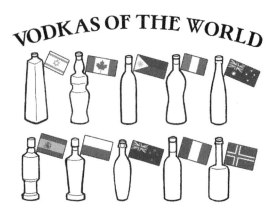

This is from *Shanken News Daily*, April 14, 2015:

> *Imported vodka continued its recent streak of dwindling volume gains in the U.S. last year, with a volume total that failed to move beyond the roughly 26.2 million cases reached in 2013, according to Impact Databank. The category's flat performance in 2014 is a dramatic departure from just a few years ago. In 2011, for example, imported vodka enjoyed double-digit growth resulting in a gain of more than 2 million cases. The category's lackluster results are coming from the top. Only one of the top five import brands grew more than 1% last year—Svedka—while the other four (Absolut, Grey Goose, Pinnacle and Ketel One) lost volume or barely advanced.*

Once upon a time, the dominant categories of choice in the United States were mainly whisk(e)y, but also gin, brandy, and liqueurs. Vodka, the easiest spirit to produce, was considered in the domain of alcohol abusers, thanks to its supposed odorless, colorless, and tasteless requirement by federal law. Then along came James Bond, followed closely by the discovery of the cocktail and the ubiquitous nature of vodka—and suddenly, everything changes.

When I worked at Yankelovich, Skelly and White—the social and political research firm—Florence Skelly had a unique way of describing the shift in preference from 'brown' liquor to vodka. She ascribed the shift as resulting from the change in values in the U.S.: from the work ethic principle, to the instant gratification attitude.

She put it this way, in a tongue-in-cheek manner: Whiskies have an acquired taste, and consumers who started drinking had to "work hard" to overcome the "silent shudder" of the first drink. When that happened, someone would say, "I know it tastes awful, but you'll get used to it, and trust me, it will have been worth the effort." She was describing traditional American values—The Work Ethic.

By the 1960s, a new generation had different values centered on instant gratification; the work ethic was no longer in play. Vodka provided the alcohol effect, and not only removed the silent shudder—the taste was actually pleasant, due to the masking effect of the mixer.

Tongue-in-cheek or not, there's some truth to it.

From a manufacturing standpoint, vodka is less expensive to produce, since there are fewer steps in the process and no aging, no barreling, no inventory sitting around taking up space and costing money. Vodka goes from still to bottle, and with higher profit margins (generally) than whiskies. That's why there are so many vodkas out there.

Thus it's not surprising that vodka dominates the spirits world. But there are storm clouds on the horizon.

*   *   *

The State of the Spirits Business

What's behind the continuing growth of liquor?

When the Distilled Spirits Council of the U.S. (DISCUS) presented its 2015 Market Report, it indicated that spirits (liquor) sales were up 4% to $24 billion, and volume grew 2.3% to 215 million cases.

In addition, market share versus beer increased for the fifth year in a row. Overall, spirits sales share went up 6.7 points since 2000, to over 35% of revenue. Most interesting to me: supplier revenue in 2015 just about doubled from 2000. Sales went from $11.7 to $24.1 billion.

The DISCUS release went on to report a number of factors contributing to the industry growth, all of which made sense. However, I have my own take on the factors and trends that are driving liquor sales; and they can be best summed up as changes in consumer attitudes and behavior.

Let's take a look at changing consumer taste preferences, with a brief trip down drinking memory lane.

From the 50s to the 70s, whiskey dominated drinking preferences. The "silent shudder" that came from the first sip of an American or Scotch whiskey was worth the effort "once you got used to it." From the 1980s to the 2000s, consumers stampeded away from whiskies into vodka, the ubiquitous alcohol that provided the kick, but was mixable with almost anything that masked or camouflaged the taste.

Over the last ten years, a new generation of drinkers has turned back to whiskey; for its perceived greater depth of flavor and its newfound mixability, thanks to the cocktail resurgence. (By the way, that desire for taste and depth of flavor is also what is driving the craft beer growth.)

The vodka suppliers also shot themselves in the foot with the flavor explosion, which went from the sublime to the ridiculous; from citrus to esoteric, from serious flavors to choices like whipped cream and marshmallow. The result has been the ability to purchase over 600 flavors— and slower growth. Vodka sales are underperforming in the overall spirits category, as a new generation of drinkers goes back to what their parents or grandparents rejected.

This consumer is asking: What's in the bottle and how did it get there?

This new generation has brought with it a conversation about the craft of making spirits, and like many changing values, the interest has spread to other age groups. While once upon a time consumers focused on the alcohol effect, today the focus is on ingredients, process, the distiller, and artistry, among a host of other manufacturing factors.

In short, certain parts of the spirits industry are becoming more akin to the wine business and craft beer, with an emphasis on quality, taste, and small batch production. In fact, DISCUS reports that small distilleries grew from 92 in 2010 to more than 750 in 2015, and from 700K cases in volume to more than 3.5 million today.

It's not about mass production or even consumption. Quality rules. Are you listening, Smirnoff and Budweiser? Run all the clever ads you like; you won't stop this trend.

Whiskey was once the domain of men, and distillers tended to shy away from marketing and advertising to women. It wasn't until 1987 that DISCUS lifted a voluntary ban on advertising directly to women. In a *Huffington Post* article, Meghan O'Dea of The Whiskey Women had this to say: "We're seeing a move toward gender-neutral drinking." (Check out her website. The home page has this slogan, which I love: "Fill your mother's crystal decanter with your father's drink of choice.")

I think the days of "girl drinks" are over. And I think that the recent tutti frutti direction in vodka is a contributing factor. Again, according to O'Dea:

Women are consciously realizing that the beverages you enjoy have a lot to say about who you are as a woman...women are shying away from drinks that infantilize them.

Clearly, whiskies have benefited from this change in attitude, and while flavored whiskey may have played a role, it's by no means the sole driving factor.

With more positive attitudes toward spirits consumption among consumers, I expect that the growth of the category will continue. DISCUS does a good job in promoting market access and helping to change archaic purchase laws. After all, how do you tell the public that state after state is legalizing marijuana, but you can't buy liquor on a Sunday?

Absolut Truth – The Beginning of the End

In January of each year at Seagram, we would meet with distributor management at a forum called the Seagram Advisory Council. The intent was to discuss the previous year, and how we looked over the holidays. It reminded me of a story about a candid assessment of a new vodka product from V&S (Absolut owners at the time) called Sundsvall.

Let me set the stage for you.

In the late 90s, it was clear that high-end, connoisseur, and sometimes "badge" vodka products were on the ascendency. From a day-to-day marketing and sales standpoint, it was also clear that Absolut was becoming a middle brand, flanked by the top shelf entries above, and the value priced vodkas below.

We requested, pleaded, and ultimately begged our Swedish partner to supply a brand that would compete with Ketel One and Grey Goose. Unfortunately, the gentleman who ran the brand at V&S was totally disinterested. His intractable position was that Absolut was the best, and to have a more expensive and presumably higher quality entry would belie their proposition.

No amount of cajoling could change his mind. We tried to explain that the analogy was in the scotch market—single malts are not better than blended scotches, they're different. He ignored his own people, those of us in the trenches, and the entreaties of Edgar Bronfman Jr.

Finally out of the blue, we were informed that a top shelf vodka brand would soon become available. I suspect that Junior went to the top of the V&S feeding chain to get it done; or for all I know, the King of Sweden himself. We didn't care, so long as we had a viable brand.

Ah "viable," what a good word. Like the cliché, it's in the eye of the beholder.

The good news: the proposition made sense and was indeed viable, including differences from Absolut in ingredients and distillation process. The up charge of $3 to $4 higher than the other super premiums was well justified, in terms of the resulting taste and initial reactions.

There were two main problems. First, V&S wanted no association between Sundsvall and Absolut, even going so far as to bypass Absolut's longtime agency (TBWA) in favor of an agency in Boston. There was no reference to Absolut anywhere in the marketing material. No opportunity for synergy or leverage. To the consumer, it was just another vodka brand.

The second and bigger problem was that the package did not live up to the super premium expectation or price point. It was, at best, blah. I remember research indicated that servers and distributors liked the taste, but felt the packaging "too plain" and "too discreet versus competition." Someone described it as "a clear bottle with an orange shrink-wrapped top." Those are the most positive things we heard.

No surprise that after a strong initial push, the brand just languished.

The scene now shifts to the Seagram Advisory Council, at some offsite location and serious winter watering hole. Don't be fooled; the invitees were the best and brightest distributor management people in the business. While the afternoons and evenings were fun, the 5 or 6-hour work sessions were grueling. This was an occasion where the supplier was on the chopping block, and got to hear about strengths and weaknesses versus competition. No BS, no holds barred, all straightforward and candid remarks.

Occasionally, there would be moments of reticence, when the distributors kind of hemmed and hawed, not wanting to offend. That's what happened when the subject of Sundsvall came up. Lots of looking at the floor.

I knew why, but needed my management to hear the problems first-hand, from our customers who obviously didn't want to offend or appear negative.

Question after question was lobbed, and the answers were platitudes and fluff. Finally, I pushed, and said, "Why is Sundsvall doing so poorly?"

One very senior manager from a very large wholesaler operation had the courage to call it like it was. He told the Absolut Truth and said, "Arthur... it's simple—the baby is ugly."

A few months later, the brand was gone. What a relief.

To this day, I believe that the V&S (the Swedish monopoly that owned the brand) senior manager, who never wanted an up market brand in the first place, did all he could to sabotage the effort. It wasn't the only mistake he made. (As you'll read about at the end of this chapter.)

Cultural Differences

A friend once told me a story of his experience doing business in Japan, and I used his story while working with the Absolut brand owners.

When we began working with our Swedish partners, they would lapse into conversations with each other in Swedish every now and then. Since their command of English was as good or better than many of ours, we were a bit dumbfounded, and unsure of what to make of it. Invariably, we were told something like, "oh, please excuse us, it's sometimes easier to share our thoughts amongst ourselves in Swedish." Sure.

On one occasion, I decided to relate a story my friend Ernie had told me about a trip to Japan, which he took to open the retail market there on behalf of Toys "R" Us.

They brought an American with them who was fluent in Japanese, and he was told not to let it be known that he was translating. His role was to quietly inform the American team of what was actually being said. The meeting was held with a leading Japanese ad agency to discuss messaging, media, and related topics. As the meeting progressed, the Japanese translator was giving sanitized answers to the American team's requests, and the American translator was providing the real statements.

When the Japanese ad people were supposedly saying "good idea," "we understand what you're looking for," and "we'll work on it," they were actually saying things like, "they don't understand the Japanese culture or people," "keep smiling and shaking your head, they will go home soon," and "we'll do what needs to be done." Ernie kept telling his translator to keep a low profile, and that his role would be revealed when the time was right.

After an entire morning of this, it was time to go to lunch. The agency execs were still making comments, and their Japanese translator kept sanitizing their remarks. Finally, the team from the States could no longer take it. As the waiter came by to take the table's order, Ernie whispered to his American translator, "now!" In fluent Japanese, this American, who had sat quietly through the meetings just taking it all in, began to order food in perfect Japanese. The agency executives turned pale and lowered their heads.

Ernie said, "Please tell them that after lunch, we will start over."

When I told this story to the people from Absolut, they just smiled and nodded their heads.

Vodkas I have known...and wish I hadn't

I was recently reminded of two attempts from Seagram to launch a vodka brand, prior to the Absolut distribution agreement. Both came at a time when the vodka category was surging, and we had no meaningful brand.

Both attempts failed.

I was running marketing for the Asia Pacific/Global Duty Free division, and like the rest of Seagram, we needed a vodka brand. By the time I got to that division, plans were well underway—a concept, package, manufacturing, sales and marketing plans, and an interesting name, Bolshoi. The brand was made in an eastern European city, and the idea was to ship it through Siberia to the port city of Vladivostok, and then on to markets in Asia.

When I got to the group, I was greeted with the marketing plan and budget. As I went over the materials to acquaint myself with what was going on, I noticed something peculiar in the shipping costs. There was an invoice for close to or over $100,000, that was over and above the actual transportation costs. It was marked "Transport Support." There was a separate line item for transportation.

I asked about it, and was told it was for a company of security guards (probably soldiers) who would accompany the initial shipment through Russia, the Urals, and Siberia. The guards were needed to make sure the shipment got there safely.

The brand did well in Asia, but was discontinued when Absolut came along. Good thing—because the cost of goods would have killed it anyway.

The other attempt involved Wyborowa from Poland. The W's are pronounced as V's, and therein lies part of the tale.

Imported vodkas in the U.S. were just beginning to make their move, and somehow we got a shot at getting the distribution of this brand with a long pedigree. It dated back to 1823, where it sold domestically, became a strong export brand throughout Europe, and became the first vodka brand to get an international trademark in 1927. Best of all, the Soviet Union dissolved, and the Poles were eager to go capitalist.

A group of us went to Poland and quickly learned what it takes to deal with a country emerging from the shadows of communism. We were at a conference table, and there were many different liquids for us to drink, as you would expect, while we discussed the prospects of doing business. Mineral water, sparkling water, spring water, even tonic. The bottles were in all different colors; some were brown, some clear, some tinted. So when you poured a liquid from a particular colored bottle (none had labels), thinking that this one was the sparkling water, it would turn out to be tonic. Our hosts made it clear that the economic difficulties meant all bottles were reused, and did not allow the "luxury" of dedicated glass.

Okay I thought, these people are doing the best they can, making do and trying to move forward despite the obstacles. Good for them.

As the discussions progressed, the issue of package size came up. They had a litre size, but the next size down was a 700ml, which is the required size in Europe. Unfortunately, that size is not legal in the U.S., which requires a 750ml. We explained that in order to sell in the off-premise trade, we needed them to produce that glass. After much whispered conversation and heated exchanges in Polish, the managing director said they had found an answer. He informed us that rather than go to the expense of new molds and glass manufacture, they would use the litre bottles and simply fill them three quarters full.

None of us laughed or revealed our amusement. It was, after all, a creative solution stemming from a difficult economic environment. We merely pointed out that the U.S. government wouldn't allow that, and joked about the interference of bureaucrats—east and west.

Turns out the production problems were solved, a new contemporary package was developed, and the brand was launched. Nothing, however, could overcome the brand name and call issue. No one wants to stand in a bar and call for a brand they can't pronounce. Ad campaigns and on-premise programming couldn't counter the verbal stumble of saying Wyborowa.

The brand does under 2 million cases around the world—most of it in Poland. The rest is in Italy, France, and Mexico. Proper pronunciation is not required.

Wacky World of Vodka

Over half a billion 9-litre cases of vodka are sold annually around the world. It should therefore come as no surprise that some strange things occur with brands, people, and the vodka category itself.

1. The Vodka for the Rich

Stoli once introduced a $3,000 bottle of vodka from the Himalayan Edition of Stolichnaya's Pristine Water Series. Only 300 bottles were sold globally. Apparently what made it so expensive was the type of water used, sourced from the Himalayan mountains, from an underground reservoir that had been pooling fresh melted snow. The water was then combined with 100% winter wheat harvested from Russia's Tambov region. As an added bonus, it came in a hand-blown glass bottle with a gold-plated decorative ice pick—perfect for your spouse to stick in your brain when he/she sees the credit card bill.

Not to be outdone, there is a company I believe is based in Hong Kong, selling (or about to launch) Royal Dragon vodka from Russia. There are three editions, but the Emperor Vodka will be made from rye, and only 888 bottles will be sold.

From their website:

This masterly hand blown Dragon caged within a pristine glass bottle is crowned with an exquisite high-end piece of jewelry. The exclusive Dragon pendant of 18-carat gold is set with perfectly shaped certified diamonds.

"Honey, I bought you some jewelry for your birthday."

2. Bad Taste Department a.k.a. "What are they thinking?"

A vodka company had planned to sponsor a party promoting a book, which discusses the experiences of two tennis stars that survived the sinking of the Titanic. The brand? Iceberg Vodka. On their website they said, "In 1912 the 'unsinkable' Titanic found that out all too tragically, we do not take our Icebergs lightly." April 15, 2012 marked the 100th anniversary of the sinking of the Titanic. They have since removed any mention of the Titanic.

In Kazakhstan, a vodka branded with the Arabic word Allah had caused an uproar in the predominantly Muslim country. The Imams in the country were outraged, and rightfully so. A representative of the company that produces the vodka denied intentional blasphemy, insisting the labels and caps are manufactured in Russia. Sure, blame the Russians.

3. New Uses for Vodka

You may have seen something like it before, but a website called Business Insider had a posting called "Awesome Ways To Use Cheap Vodka Around The House." My favorites: getting rid of mold; air freshener when mixed with water and sprayed; preventing flowers from wilting (and making them happier); polish and shine (as a replacement for window cleaners). The best: treat dandruff by mixing one cup vodka with two teaspoons crushed rosemary, then strain the mixture through a coffee cup filter and let it sit for two days before applying it to your head and letting the solution dry.

The key is to use inexpensive vodka, unless you can afford a $3,000 bottle of Stoli.

By the way, does the Stoli come with someone to serve the vodka?

Who Stole the Vodka? Better Question – Why Bother?

The Buffalo Trace Newsletter—*Industry News Update*—had an article about the theft of $1.1 million worth of vodka (752 cases) from a customs warehouse in Miami.

According to a number of news reports, including *CNN*:

The men were caught by the cameras loading... several boxes containing Spirits of the Tsars Golden Vodka, a Ukrainian-made vodka that features 24-carat gold on its label that retails for between U.S. $250 in the off-trade and $1,200 in the on-trade.

The product is "golden" not just because of the label; it is an amber color aged in Cognac barrels for three years.

A number of observations come to mind.

According to the label, this is not vodka but a vodka specialty—"vodka infused with grape wine brandy and natural flavors with caramel color." At $250 a bottle, the closest you get to Cognac is the barrel? "Golden" vodka, thanks to caramel coloring? Where are you when we need you, P.T. Barnum?

Most thefts of liquor generally involve product placement under the raincoat, or "slippage" out the back door. That's why you see expensive products in lock boxes, behind the counter, or with a "chastity belt" around the cap. But these thieves punched a hole in the wall of the warehouse directly to the area where the vodka was stored. They win the award for brazenness, as well as stupidity. Who is going to buy the vodka? Their sales are small, so an appearance of these goods will be noticed.

[Can you picture this? Somewhere in the basement of a garish McMansion sits a retired oligarch who ushers his guests into a special wood paneled room, where they sip this golden elixir while admiring a stolen Picasso.]

The response from the company was to offer a reward worth $5,000. At $1.1 million, 752 cases means it's worth $1,462 per case. As *CNN* put it, "if you use that reward to buy the stuff at some South Beach nightclubs, you could buy about four bottles of it."

The chincy reward makes me wonder. But then again, the name of the game in the Booze Business is depletions of stock—through the front door preferably, but any other way would also work.

Anyone with information about this theft is urged to stop laughing.

Mary Jane's Primo Hemp Vodka: Booze Meets Grass

What do you think about Vodka made with hemp?

TO DO OR NOT TO DO?

Well there is one, and it's called Mary Jane's Primo Hemp Vodka, on sale in Canada.

With the legalization of marijuana in a number of states, many wonder which state will be up next in going pro-cannabis. Let's look at another approach.

An entrepreneur in Canada named S.R. Collier (founder and CEO) developed a vodka brand with a 4.20% infusion of hemp, which is introduced during distillation. That negligible amount of THC (the chemical responsible for marijuana's psychoactive effect) and the distillation process do not affect the buzz, but rather give the brand some "fun, naughty, and interesting marketing hype," according to Mr. Collier. I have not had the opportunity to try it; but from what I am told, it provides a distinctive and unique taste with overtones of hazelnut. Collier explains that the hemp oil yields an "ultra smooth" profile.

Are you wondering why this Mary Jane Vodka isn't available in the United States? Enter the alcohol regulatory authority.

The product was submitted to the Alcohol and Tobacco Tax and Trade Bureau (TTB) for formula and label approval. The formula was approved, but due to the label containing the image and phrase "Mary Jane" (slang for marijuana), the product was ultimately rejected. Who knew the TTB was so hip?

But wait a minute. This is the same regulatory agency that approved alcohol labels with such names as Fokker Ale, Fuchen Liqueur, Chockin' Chicken, Fat Bastard, Big Dick Beer, along with other classy names. Never mind—Mary Jane's Primo Hemp Vodka cannot be sold in the U.S. under that name. But the product itself is okay.

Introducing Washington's Revolution Spirit.

It turns out that our founding fathers (Washington and Jefferson included) grew hemp on their farms. The crop was useful for rope, paper, and clothing. Hemp was long promoted in Virginia as an alternative cash crop to tobacco. According to some sources, Washington not only grew hemp, but also actively promoted its growth. Allegedly, in a letter to his plantation field manager, he wrote, "Make the most of the Indian hemp seed... and sow it everywhere!"

So Mr. Collier has changed the name of his product to Washington's Revolution Spirit for U.S. distribution. The TTB approved that label, and it uses the Mary Jane's Primo Hemp Vodka formulation currently used in Canada. Same recipe, different name.

*   *   *

Flavored vodkas

Pinnacle Vodka boasts more than 40 flavors, including Whipped Cream, Cinnabon, Caramel Apple, Key Lime Pie, Cookie Dough, and other sure-to-make-you-gag flavors.

When I think about the crazy flavor direction in vodka, a few thoughts spring to mind, such as: who drinks this chemically derived crap? Why? The flavor houses must be making a bundle.

There is also the business side. When you're running a booze company with Wall Street and stock price scrutiny, you do your utmost to make your numbers. Often it's difficult to grow and meet expectations with the current stable of brands.

Line extensions in the form of flavored vodkas give the balance sheet a nice (albeit temporary) boost.

In other words, fad products are good for business. Unless of course, you're a retailer stuck with the favor-of-the-day inventory.

*   *   *

A final word about Absolut

Just how did this brand become an icon, and then ultimately lose its luster?

The gentleman who was given the mission by the V&S Company in Sweden to make Absolut a global brand (which in those days, meant the U.S.), was an engineer, not particularly well-versed in marketing matters. He was responsible for the design and package, but struggled for many years to gain acceptance for the brand. Eventually, he met Michel Roux, who loved the idea; Roux found TBWA and the Absolut campaign was born. The success was so pronounced, the brand became an icon and sales took off. At periodic review and approval meetings, the "brand owner" (V&S) had little say in the direction of the brand. Oh, I suppose on paper they could call the shots, but Michel Roux was a tour de force—and come on, who's going to rock the successful boat? Especially if you work in a state monopoly and have to deal with a powerhouse marketer like Michel.

The scene shifts: Michel and his parent company lose the distribution rights to Seagram. This time, the Swedes started to flex their muscles a bit more. Unlike the freewheeling entrepreneur-esque manner of Michel Roux, the Swedes confronted what they called the Seagram "machine." They tried to get the upper hand, but at the end of the day, the engineer and his people had to concede the growth at Seagram was as good or better than with Roux. Plus, the brand's equity was protected and enhanced. Under Michel Roux, Absolut's growth was concentrated on the coasts. At Seagram, that strength was maintained but suddenly the brand developed strong followers in the middle of the country. It had become a national brand and grew by double digits every month for years.

The engineer retired, and was replaced by a well-intentioned but pompous and intractable executive. This new V&S leader of Absolut knew little about marketing, and nothing about the U.S. vodka market. Despite the gains made by the Seagram team, he was determined to be the shining light of the company success, and made it clear that we would follow his rules and wishes. Everything became a battle.

"No, that event is wrong and not in the brand's image." Huh? We've been doing this for some time, attracted new consumers, and the return on the brand's investment has been strong. "Absolut will not be associated with the gay market." Nonsense; the gay community is just one of the diverse markets in the U.S. Besides, Absolut is strong there, and we need to support gay causes. Fortunately, we won that battle—but grudgingly, on his part.

The biggest mistake came from the stubborn reluctance to counter Grey Goose and Ketel One until it was too late; and then, only with a half-assed effort, as previously described.

But the ultimate act of folly came when Seagram closed. V&S owned the brand; it was now a private, non-government company, who decided to go it alone in the U.S. with a wholly owned U.S. entity. The Swedish managing director didn't do enough fact checking on the Seagram alumnus chosen to lead their U.S. operation. He was a good golfer, but didn't do much for Absolut.

Long story short, Absolut started to falter, and they didn't know how to fix it. They joined forces with a large spirits company, but it didn't help. They forced the bungling manager out, cleaned house, and brought in a top-notch executive. But it was too late.

Ultimately, the Absolut brand got sold to Pernod Ricard for $18 billion. This is an excellent spirits and wine company that is hugely successful, and employs very smart people. The jury is still out as to whether they will be able to bring the brand back. I suppose if anyone can do it, Pernod Ricard can.

*   *   *

There are those who relate the Absolut initial success to the power of the TBWA/Chiat advertising campaign. It was spectacular and truly iconic advertising.

But there are some (including me) that trace the initial impetus of the brand to global politics and the Cold War. The ad campaign played a supporting role.

In the early 1980s, Russian misadventures caused quite a stir. The invasion of Afghanistan in 1979 led to the U.S. boycott of the Olympics in Moscow. The shooting down of KAL 007 in 1983 followed that. Boycotts of Russian products were widespread all over the world, but especially in the U.S., with a focus on the Russian vodka, Stolichnaya (Stoli). Newspaper tabloids ran many photos of bartenders pouring Stoli down sewers.

At the time, domestic products dominated the vodka market, and only three imports were available. The clear choice among the imported vodka-leaning segment of drinkers was Stoli. Absolut and Finlandia were the other two, both very weak brands. When the boycotts took place, the imported vodka crowd leaned toward Absolut. What was heretofore seen as an inappropriate apothecary bottle became a sign of authenticity. The brand was discovered, and the ad campaign added to the allure.

*   *   *

9. Marketing vs. sales—Let the games begin

I prefer being a salesperson to being a marketer.

In marketing, you come up with a strategy, a communications plan, an advertising campaign, whatever. You like it, others don't. You hate it, your colleagues think it's great. There is lots of room for interpretation, opinions, and disparate reactions in the marketing world.

In sales, you can't be a little bit pregnant. You either make the sale or you don't. There's nothing in between.

A marketing plan doesn't bring in business the same way as selling a truckload of merchandise does. I suppose that I'm a marketer at heart, but realistic enough to know that often, marketing's most important function is to support sales.

Historically, in the post-WWII period and throughout the 1960s, the spirits and wine industry was sales dominant. Demand exceeded supply; there were few significant and large companies; distribution ruled. By the 1970s, the picture had changed, and the consumer ruled. Shifts in the industry created an environment whereby supply exceeded demand.

Consumer package goods businesses, including the **Booze Business**, turned to the brand management system and concentrated on marketing as the most important element. It started at Procter & Gamble and spread throughout business.

From *Brand Strategy Insider*:

After its successes with Ivory and Crisco, P&G developed a new business technique called "brand management." Because it focused attention on a product rather than a business function, brand management turned out to be similar in its effects to the multi-divisional structure introduced by Alfred Sloan at General Motors. And it had the same powerful tendency to decentralize decision-making.

It's therefore not surprising that Seagram adopted the brand management system in the late 1970s/early 1980s. With that system, came an emphasis on marketing disciplines—an emphasis on brand building, advertising, "pull" over "push," and other out of store efforts—at the expense of the single-minded focus on sales.

For the most part, it worked. But the **Booze Business** is not like the laundry detergent business. The mandatory 3-tier system and the emphasis on the distributor (the middle man) meant that it didn't work smoothly.

First, the natural antithesis between sales and marketing accelerated and got worse. As time went on, turf protection and budget battles became common elements of brand and business planning. Second, an unhealthy "us vs. them" atmosphere prevailed, and became exasperated as many brand managers focused on planning at their desks and lost touch with the street, the store, and the consumer. Going to a focus group and eating M&M's replaced hands-on market visits.

The sales people realized there just might be something to this marketing stuff, after all. At the very least, it seemed important, since that's where the budgets were going. Having sales people start thinking about marketing and marketing programing at the regional and local level was a good thing. Although there were times when marketing people would shrug, and ask, "when did a t-shirt become a strategy?"

When I ran marketing for U.S., I had a department of 120 people and a central budget of close to $150 million. With brands that needed strong marketing strategies and executions, I was very caught up in the notion of central marketing laying the course that sales and related activities needed to follow.

As I look back on it, with what I know now, I would have pushed for a different approach. The simple fact of the matter is that marketing in the spirits world is basically sales support. For an enterprise (alcohol or not) to succeed, both disciplines need to work in tandem. To a large extent, marketing can only be effective if the sales team can gain distribution and store presence.

A friend of mine put it this way: marketing people may be smarter, but sales people are more fun.

As you're about to find out.

*   *   *

Salesman in Winter

A salesman for one of the Seagram sales companies called on bars in Wisconsin in the dead of winter. His main objective was to get Kessler Blended Whiskey placed. His mission, his bonus, and perhaps even his job depended on sufficient sales of the brand. Not easy, since Wisconsin was (and still is) a market cluttered with whiskies and brandies.

He would park his car out front, walk into the bar, engage the owner/manager, and talk about the virtues of Kessler. Invariably, the bar owner would tell him that he already had enough whiskies, and no room or interest in a new one.

To overcome the owner/manager resistance, his spiel was always the same. "Listen, this brand is so distinctive and stands out from other whiskies, that I'll bet you I can pick Kessler out of a line-up of whatever whiskies you care to test it against. I'll get a bottle and you can pour a shot of it, and any other whiskies, and I'll always be able to pick the Kessler."

Now baited, the owner would likely say, "What's the bet?" The salesman's answer would be something like "50 bucks if I can't pick it, and you buy 3 bottles if I can." Hardly anyone turned him down.

He would go out to his car, bring in a bottle, give it to the owner, and turn his back. The owner would pour shot glasses for the "taste test," including any number of brands, plus a shot of Kessler.

The salesman would turn around and take a sip of each whiskey; then very quickly point to the shot of Kessler and say, "that's it." He was never wrong. Always got the sale, up and down the state of Wisconsin.

How did he do it?

Since it had just come from the trunk of his car, it was the only one that was cold.

To this day, Kessler is still a very strong blended whiskey brand, whose main strength is in Wisconsin.

"Why are we more boozy?"

"Upper Midwesterners drink more. Could it be our northern European roots? The weather?"

A story with these words appear on the website of the Twin Cities' *Star Tribune*.

The story reported that Minnesota is one of the top 5 drinking states in the U.S. Experts point out part of the explanation is that many residents in the upper Midwest are descendants from countries with high alcohol consumption. Another reason given, of course, is the long cold winters and indoor activity that goes nicely with alcohol consumption.

Jerry Mann once told me about a sales trip he made to the upper Midwest. As someone who grew up in more moderate winter climates, he was a bit out of his element.

After a long, bitterly cold day north of Minneapolis, he decided to call it a day and drive to the hotel he had booked for the night. He checked in, dropped his suitcase, and immediately headed for the bar. He figured it was early, so he'd check the brands on the back shelf, order a drink, and chat with the bartender.

While he sipped on his Seagram's Gin on the rocks, he introduced himself to the bartender, and a conversation ensued. The first question Jerry asked was about the parking garage.

"Listen pal," Jerry starts off. "I noticed when I pulled into the garage, there were all these wires hanging from the ceiling that look like electric plugs. What's that all about?"

"How long ago was that?" asked the barman.

"About 5, maybe 10 minutes ago," the salesman replied.

The barman says, in a very Midwest accent, "Those are for engine block heating, and they connect to the engine to keep it from freezing. Most of the cars up here, especially rentals, have a plug to connect to them. I hope you used it."

"Oh hell," said Jerry as he got up to leave. "I didn't know... I'll be right back."

The barman stared at him, smiled, and said, "Forget about it. It's too late now."

Jerry sat down, took out a cigarette, lit it, and took a puff. He smiled at the barman and said, "Well in that case, make this a double."

Retailer Incentives

I was hired as the VP, Market Research from outside the booze industry. Bright-eyed and bushy-tailed, I decided that I was going to learn the business by talking to consumers, retailers, and the sales people on the street.

For weeks, I did nothing but visit market after market, and rode along with local sales managers. I learned a great deal in the field, more than I would have by sitting at a desk and listening to presentations.

Among other things, I learned that the business is based on relationships, and for the most part, respect between the buyer and seller. The trip taught me how the 3-tier system works, how the consumer needs to be factored into the equation, and the difference between a smart sales rep and one that's just going through the motions.

The plan was to see as wide and diverse a set of retail situations as possible; bars at night and stores during the day. Some open-ended consumer focus groups were thrown in here and there, just for the learning.

One day I found myself in Detroit. The morning was spent in suburban stores and the afternoon was devoted to downtown. The local sales manager for the company was among the best, really knew his stuff.

A new word entered my vocabulary: "bank" store. Those are stores in tough urban settings with thick Plexiglas separating the clerks and the customers.

At one large, important account, the owner greeted the sales rep warmly. With a Middle Eastern accent, the owner said, "How are you? What do you have for me today?"

"We have a Seagram's Gin program coming up that you might want to look into," said the salesman.

"What will I get?" asked the owner. "Never mind," he quickly added, "I don't need to promote gin. What's in your bag? Any t-shirts or hats?"

"No; just shelf talkers, window ads, banners, and sales sheets."

"Paper," said the owner. "I don't need no paper. Got any more Captain Morgan mirrors? My father-in-law saw one in the store and took it home. I want one, too."

"I'm sorry," said the salesman. "That program ended months ago; it was so successful, we ran out."

"What do you have in the trunk of your car?" asked the storeowner.

By now, I was watching this interchange with amazement.

"Listen, I'm just showing this gentleman from New York around the market and into different stores. You're an important account for us, and I wanted him to see it. I don't have sales promotion or loader items. Maybe next time."

"Sure, sure," said the storeowner. "What do you have in your trunk?"

"Nothing."

"Come on, come on, what's in the trunk?" asked the retailer.

With total poise and calm, the salesman handed his car keys to the owner, and said, "check for yourself."

He went on, "but this time leave the spare tire."

Godiva Liqueur

It took years to get the owners of Godiva Chocolatier to license the brand for a chocolate liqueur. It took a lot less time to learn that building the brand would not be easy.

Despite the absence of a meaningful liqueur in the portfolio, distribution was slow; since liqueurs are not a fast moving category, the turnover rate was even slower.

There's a great story of a Seagram sales executive who goes to a Chinese restaurant on Long Island, and while he and his family are waiting for a table, spots a bottle of Godiva on the back bar. This is the last type of restaurant he would expect to find the product, and figures that the distributor sales rep who sold the account must be at the top of his game. What could he have said about the brand that got this small neighborhood restaurant to order it?

He goes up to the owner and says, "What did the salesman tell you to get you to take in the Godiva?" The owner looked a bit puzzled at first, then smiled, and said in a thick Cantonese accent, "Oh, he say two free vodkas if I buy the Godiva."

After much research and thought, we came to the conclusion that despite the power of the brand name, there was a discontinuity between the expectation of the chocolate taste and the delivery of the product. When you say "chocolate" to people, they think, chewy, sweet, and unique "mouth feel." This is hard to deliver in a liquid product without ending up gloppy. So for many, the expectation was chocolate—but the product delivered a Kahlua-like consistency.

We had to move out of the chocolate-only world and get closer to cream liqueurs. Two line extensions were introduced; a cappuccino/chocolate and a white chocolate, both cream products.

These strategic line extensions had a number of benefits. First, the facings went from 2 to 6, and the billboard effect on the shelf got the brand noticed and bought. Second, despite the old adage not to line extend from weakness—line extensions are best when the parent brand is strong—the new forms actually benefitted the base brand (original), which started to grow. A brand that was languishing in the 10,000 cases range grew to nearly 40,000. After Diageo got it, it grew to over 100,000 cases.

So if you see a bottle of Godiva on the back bar of any Chinese restaurant on Long Island, I bet it's been there since 1995.

Where's the alcohol section?

A former Seagram colleague went to work for a company known as Allied Domecq. At the time, this company was based in the U.K., and many of their marketing people had little to no clue what it was like doing business in the U.S.

It seems they weren't very happy with the way their brands were being run in the States (New York in particular), and one of their top-ranking marketing people was coming over for a series of meetings to discuss reasons for the poor performance.

A senior member of the NY sales team met the executive at the airport when he came through customs. He ushered him to his car, and told him the plan for the first day was to bring him to the hotel, get settled, and then tour the market.

"I hope to see stores as they really are, and not have one of your set-up visits," said the marketing guy. To which the sales person replied, "any store you like...you're staying in Manhattan, so lets start there. You choose."

A few minutes went by, and the visitor exclaimed that he needed to go to a drugstore right away. "Please find one close by."

Thinking that he must have had a headache or some other physical ailment from the flight, the salesman pulled off the expressway and stopped at the first chain drugstore he saw.

He was gone for about 10 minutes, then came storming out, got back into the car, and complained loudly and bitterly that he had looked all over the store and didn't find any of their brands.

The salesman patiently explained that in NY, the sale of alcohol was not allowed in drugstores.

"But it is allowed in other states, isn't it?"

"Yes, in a few states," said the salesman.

"So if you and your associates weren't so damn lazy, you'd get the law changed, wouldn't you?"

The salesman didn't bother to explain.

Distributor Sales Rep

The Wine & Spirits Wholesalers of America (WSWA) is the national trade association representing the wholesale tier of the wine and spirits industry. It is dedicated to advancing the interests and independence of wholesale distributors and brokers of wine and spirits.

There have been lots of changes in the second tier—the wholesaler/distributor level—over the past few decades. From marketing to logistics to the people on the street, spirits wholesaler operations have become much more professional.

But it wasn't always that way.

The gentleman who told me about this next incident was working for Seagram in Massachusetts in the 1980s, when the 375 Spirits Co. (one of the Seagram companies) introduced Mumm Cognac. The idea was to use their Champagne credentials to enter the highly profitable Cognac business. In typical Seagram fashion, the new product introduction to wholesalers was an elaborate affair held in a hotel ballroom, complete with a French-themed dinner.

After dinner, the team got down to the business of introducing the product to the distributor sales people. The focus was on the quality, romance, and story of selling a cognac with the specialness of the Mumm name. They educated the sales people on the geography of the Cognac region, the type of grapes used, the distillation process, and the magic of aging, using terms likes Angel's Share, Grande Champagne *eaux de vie*, quality grade differences, etc.

After an extensive tasting session, with emphasis on the different characteristics of such a high quality product, the salesmen were asked if they had any questions. One hand went up. It was from a salesman who had been in the business for years. "Yes, Irving, what is your question?"

"Does this shit come in half gallons?"

"DOES THIS SHIT COME IN HALF GALLONS?"

Selecting a Wine for Thanksgiving

A husband and wife are walking back and forth in the wine section just before Thanksgiving. They are obviously having a hard time deciding what to buy.

At a different time and place, somewhere in the world, the owners of a vineyard have worried about the harvest, pressing, fermentation, testing, blending, fining, filtration, bottling, and a dozen other things that the vintner and owners are concerned about. They taste, refine, and taste again. On and on it goes, until they are satisfied. A great wine is born.

At the same time, the marketing and sales people are concerning themselves with the name, packaging, and brand identity. They fuss over the label; they agonize about the back label copy; they pray for good reviews.

We now return to the retail shop where this wine is on the shelf. Our consumer couple is staring blankly at the shelves. We eavesdrop on their conversation:

He: What difference does it make? Pick one.

She: I'm confused. Should we pick it by price? Or based on these little cards with ratings?

He: I don't know. Price doesn't always mean anything. Do you know what the Johnsons like?

She: No idea. Let's ask the sales guy.

He: Are you kidding? Does he look like he knows anything about wine? I might ask him about beer, but... It's like asking for directions. Forget it. Let's decide ourselves.

She: How about this one? It's a cute name.

He: Dancing Elves? Looks more like Fornicating Elves to me.

She: If it were up to you, you'd probably pick Farting Bears.

He: Okay. Enough. Just pick one.

She: I got it. Look at this bottle. It's all in earth tones. Marge's dining room décor is orange, yellow, and brown—this one will match her table setting!

He: Great. Let's go. The game starts soon.

Somewhere in the world, there is the sound of gunfire. Another vintner has blown his brains out.

Diversity Booze – Who Drinks What and Why?

I saw an article in *Wine & Spirits Daily* titled, "Capitalizing on the Growing Ethnic Trend."

The article included data on the growth rates and buying power of the Latino, African-American, and Asian consumer markets. It also reported on data gathered by Republic National Distributing Company (RNDC), and described who drinks what.

Some of the reported drinking habits are well known to spirits marketers, and some show shifts from the past.

A few highlights from the article:

- Everyone drinks vodka.

- Latino consumers primarily drink beer, followed by tequila and rum.

- African-American consumers drink rum, cognac, and gin primarily; but tequila is up there in consumption.

- Asian consumers show a preference for scotch.

What I find most interesting is that compared to the past, when there were some diverse drinking preferences, now *everyone drinks everything*. There are differences, but not as drastic as those I saw years ago.

So permit me to add some comments and cautions concerning marketing to diverse population segments.

Let's begin with the diversity within diverse markets. Take the Latino or Hispanic market: It is a diverse group of consumers, consisting of people from Mexico, Puerto Rico, Central America, Cuba, and other Caribbean Islands. These sub-segments are geographically dispersed, so the Mexican American consumers in Texas, for example, are different from those in Chicago or LA.

The African-American consumer category and brand preferences also vary by geography and urban, suburban, and rural residency.

Along with that, the "Asian" category doesn't account for consumers from China, South Korea, Philippines, or other countries that have their own culture and customs.

The point is, a smart brand builder pays attention to diverse consumer markets as a starting point, but understands that further knowledge is also necessary.

Let me share a memorable experience in ethnic marketing research.

I was conducting focus groups on behalf of Patron Tequila, when Seagram had the brand. The research was among Anglo and Mexican American consumers. At the time, Patron was only just beginning to grow, and we wanted to learn attitudes and perceptions about the brand.

Many Anglo consumers told us that their favorite brands were those they believed to be "authentic" tequilas; brands like Cazadores and Herradura were mentioned. But so was Patron.

At the time, Patron was not available in Mexico (except for duty free), and it was only an export product. Yet its name and packaging made it "authentic" tequila.

Among Mexican American consumers, the attitudes became even more telling. Those who strongly maintained their Mexican identity stuck with brand preferences from "back home." But second and third-generation Mexican Americans (those more assimilated, rather than acculturated) also added Patron to their repertoire. When challenged on the lack of heritage for Patron, the most frequent reply was, "Hey, my Anglo friends drink it, so it must be good."

Looking at the market from a diversity standpoint is great—but it's critical to remember that there are many layers to a culture, and one size doesn't fit all.

Marketing is Dead – Long Live Marketing

Harvard Business Review published an article on their blog called "Marketing is Dead," written by Bill Lee, President of the Lee Consulting Group.

His view of marketing is that the "traditional" definition and tools are no longer appropriate to this new environment. Let's take a look at his evidence, which consists of three areas.

First, as Mr. Lee puts it, the "buyer's decision journey" has changed from passive information coming to consumers (amidst tens of thousands of communications a day) to interactive information gathering requested by consumers. The traditional journey—beginning with awareness and familiarity—continues, but now those decision steps are based on Internet searches, word-of-mouth, consumer reviews, and other people-to-people efforts.

Lee's second point hits at the heart of being a CMO (chief marketing officer). He cites a 2011 global study of CEOs and decision makers by a London company called Fournaise Marketing Group, which shows a significant loss of patience in marketing. Check out these survey results: 73% said CMOs "lack business credibility and are not the business growth generators they should be." (Ouch.) 72% agreed that CMOs are always asking for more money, but rarely explain how it will generate more business. Most devastating of all, 77% of those surveyed are "tired of all the talk about brand equity" and how this relates to financial equity. (Double Ouch.)

It seems to me that CMOs all over the world are using old language to explain what is really "share of mind," but are stuck on the word "equity" from 20 years ago. CEOs are looking at market expenditures and thinking about costs, when they should be thinking investment.

Finally, Lee presents the notion that the traditional marketing process is out of date, since the people behind it (agencies, business partners, consultants, etc.) don't always relate to the consumer, and tend to suggest ideas that are not relevant. (It reminds me of the David Ogilvy quote, "The consumer isn't a moron, she's your wife.")

However, I don't agree about his criticism of the marketing process. The quality of marketing is a function of the vision and leadership of the CMO. Whether traditional or new, "a fish stinks from the head down."

Whether you agree with Mr. Lee or not, there are fundamental changes underway in marketing. I buy into his view of the future. It's all about authenticity via people-to-people marketing, including peer influence, community-oriented marketing, and customer relationships.

In the **Booze Business**, we've always known about the influencer role in brand choice. Choices that are based on "I'll have what he's having," "What do you recommend?" and "What's the story behind that brand?"

*   *   *

My all-time favorite salesman story takes place in the 1950s...

There was a wiseass salesman at Seagram in Boston during a snowstorm. In those days, a hat was an important part of a gentleman's attire, and unfortunately his hat—his favorite, by the way—blew off. He chased it down the street to no avail, as the wind carried it into a slush-laden road and a snowplow demolished it.

Undeterred, he went into a hat store (yes, they had them in those days) and bought a new hat to the tune of $25 (probably over $300 today). Since the incident occurred while traveling on business, he felt it appropriate for him to add it to his reimbursable expenses. Upon his return to New York, he submitted a report for $525; including $25 for a new hat, labeled as such.

His boss calls him into his office a day later, and said angrily, "I went over your expense report—what's this about a new hat?" The salesman explained. The boss said, "That's bullshit. We're not paying for your hat. It's your problem. Redo this expense report."

The sales guy came back fifteen minutes later and handed the boss a new report.

The boss looked at it and said, "How can this be? The expenses still come to $525." The salesman looked at him, smiled and said, "I know. Bet you can't find the hat."

10. Booze Abroad—I want to go home

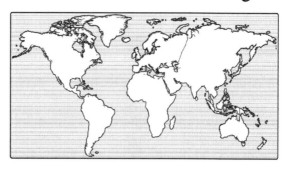

I've had more than my share of **Booze Business** dealings around the world.

After running New Product Development in the U.S. for three years, my performance ratings were such that I came to the attention of HR and global management. I loved the new products job, and could have done it forever; but the company thought they'd be doing me a favor by promoting me to Senior Vice President, Marketing for the Asia-Pacific/Global Duty Free division. I hated it.

At that time, I didn't have to relocate to Asia—Hong Kong, to be exact. If I had been forced to, I would have left the company. The corporate culture at the time was such that if you were told to relocate, and asked to talk it over with your spouse, the answer was expected to be, "All I need to discuss is whether he/she wants a window or aisle seat." I turned down a number of relocation "opportunities," and would happily have done so with a posting overseas.

But I was assured that I could still live in the NY area, and travel to Asia a few times a month. Right. I would leave on a Friday and stay through another weekend, so I was spending two weeks a month "in country."

This was only part of the problem. The man I worked for was certifiable. I thought of him as Captain Queeg of The Caine Mutiny. He was the worst manager I ever met, and he had a mean, villainous streak. After 4 months, I let my friends in HR know that if I couldn't get out from under him, I would have to leave.

I got lucky, and was appointed the Executive Vice President of marketing for the House of Seagram (U.S.). The bonus was working for Steve Kalagher, the CEO, and a very smart and likeable leader. Shortly thereafter, that division became Seagram Americas, and I had responsibility for countries from Canada to Chile. Literally.

My last international foray, which ran from 2011 to 2014, was with the APU Joint Stock Company located in Ulaanbaatar (or Ulan Bator), Mongolia. How many people do you know who have been to Mongolia on not one, but three separate occasions?

*   *   *

It all began with James Espey (whom you've met before), truly a global executive. He became an advisor to the Chairman of the APU. This company at the time was looking to grow its capabilities, and turned to James for advice and counsel. Among their needs was developing a world- class marketing department; and I was hired to go to Mongolia and spend a week lecturing on the topic.

Roughly a year later, I was hired to run the U.S. portion of their global expansion. That lasted two years.

What began with much promise and high expectation ended abruptly and sadly.

*   *   *

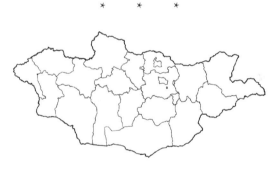

Mongolian Awakens – Part One

In 2011 I made my first a trip to Mongolia. I was consulting with the country's largest beverage company on the topic of best practices in global marketing.

Here are some first impressions—particularly because most people have only a vague and hazy image of Mongolia. As did I, before I went there.

In my view, despite its size and having only a few decades of free market economics, the country will eventually take its place among the most important emerging nations in the world. One of my colleagues who has also been there said, "They should put up a billboard over the country saying, 'watch this space.'"

I like to think of Mongolia as a "sleeping beauty." The country was put to sleep by an evil empire for 70 years, but its recent awakening foreshadows a strong new beginning.

When one thinks of Mongolia, chances are the first thing that comes to mind is the Mongol Empire and "Genghis" Khan. (In fact, it's pronounced Chinggis; Arabs could not pronounce the ch sound, and that's how it became a g sound.). By the way, the Mongol Empire had the largest contiguous land empire in history; 22% of the Earth's total known land area.

This small country that once ruled much of the world became the Mongolian People's Republic in 1924, and was subjected to Soviet rule. Suddenly, with the collapse of the evil empire in 1991, Mongolia was on its own. What followed was roughly a decade of restructuring, embrace of free market economics—and unfortunately, a deep recessionary period.

Fast-forward ten years. Despite ups and downs, the country got back on its feet; and by 2009, analysts were referring to Mongolia as the Mongolian Wolf. The untapped mineral deposits and a bourgeoning financial system made Mongolia look like the next Asian tiger. On his trip to Asia in 2011, Vice President Biden visited China, Japan, and—you guessed it—Mongolia. That ought to tell you something.

Consider this: not only is Mongolia land-locked, it's the only country I can think of that is surrounded by two super powers (Russia and China), and is dependent on them for trade and access to the world. Yet at the time I was there, the country's GDP growth was among the fastest in the world.

Roughly half the population lives in the capital of Ulaanbaatar (Ulan Bator or UB), a bustling, sprawling city struggling to keep up with the growth of the economy. As my Texan friends would say, "too many tires and not enough road." It's a city in transition, with contrasts between vestiges of the Soviet days and modern skyscrapers.

The other contrast is the perception of Mongolia versus the reality. I think visitors are surprised to see the burgeoning affluence and palpable level of optimism and aspiration there. The roads are full (perhaps too full) of late model cars, supermarket shelves are stocked with choices more extensive than many places in the States, and the modern department stores were already crowded with holiday shoppers when I visited in early November.

At one of my training sessions, we were discussing brand awareness and the importance of top-of-mind recall. I asked for people to call out names of the first automobiles that came to mind. I fully expected to hear Toyota and Hyundai, thinking those everyday brands would top the list. Instead, I got rousing choruses of Mercedes and BMW, with a few Bentleys thrown in.

That, my friends, is aspiration.

Impressions of Mongolia — Part Two

The flight to Ulan Bator from New York is long and tiring, and business class only partially eases the burden. But for this experience, it was well worth the effort.

When I stepped out of the airport and into Mongolia for the first time, there were a number of prominent impressions. First, it was cold. It was November 13th, and already below zero. I couldn't care less if it's Celsius or Fahrenheit—it's still cold! Oddly enough, by the end of the week, I was used to it. I also came to realize that people who endure such weather extremes can also endure whatever life and history throws at them.

Second, the pollution there is strong. No worse than major eastern European, South American, or Asian cities, but somehow different. There was an odor I could not identify, that I later learned was from coal. The city has a very large *ger* district, where the residents use coal for heat. (A *ger* is a felt-lined tent covered in durable, waterproof, white canvas. While modern and expensive homes are being built in UB, many rural Mongolians have retained their traditional lifestyle, of which the *ger* is an integral part.) The situation is not helped by UB's topography—it's almost completely surrounded by low mountains that trap the air until a strong wind can blow it away. Kind of like Los Angeles.

My third impression, which I got as soon as I landed, was about the people. While waiting for my luggage, I looked around and realized I could be anywhere in the world. There were lots of westerners (British, Canadians, Americans, Germans), some going home and many there on business.

But what struck me most was the pleasant demeanor of the Mongolians. Despite the waiting and the anxiety of baggage claim (or is that just me?) all I saw were smiling, happy people. To a large extent, my strongest and most favorable impression of the country was the people; warm, friendly, industrious, and very smart. I began to wonder how I could be effective as a marketing lecturer.

The city of Ulan Bator made me think of Paris in the reverse. I love Paris, but I'm not always sure about the people. In UB, I love the people, but the infrastructure needs some work. The roads are always congested, which makes me think of of São Paolo, Brazil, where a red light is only a suggestion. UB is no worse, and certainly much safer.

The problem is clear: the infrastructure has not kept pace with the city's growing affluence and economic well-being. Furthermore, the weather wreaks havoc with the streets and roads, and I'll never complain about NYC potholes again.

The weather also inhibits construction. All around the city, there are buildings going up, but I didn't see anyone working on them. It seems that due to the sub-zero weather, construction stops in the fall and resumes in the spring. I suppose it has something to do with the cement and concrete versus the weather.

Besides that, UB is an interesting, bustling metropolis with shops, restaurants, and culture reflective of Mongolia's past and present. I didn't have time for much shopping or sightseeing, but I can attest to the fact that the food was very good. Let me put it to you this way: whether Mongolian, Japanese, German, Korean, or French, I didn't meet a meal I didn't like. Then again, that might have been a result of the people I ate with, more so than the food.

*　　*　　*

Good night Mongolia

I was hired by the APU Joint Stock Company to manage the introduction and launch of their Soyombo Super Premium Mongolian Vodka in the U.S. The project began in late 2012 and ended in late 2014, with their exit from the global export business.

APU is the largest beverage company in Mongolia, and the initials translate to Vodka, Beer, and Soft drinks.

The export operation began well before I got there, but didn't move along smoothly until James Espey found Jett Yang—who took over the operation as Managing Director, Global Sales and Marketing in September 2012. I've met many executives in my time, but Jett is among the best. His background includes Japan Tobacco Company, International Distillers and Vintners (now Diageo), and major global marketing and sales positions with Bacardi. Jett is way more than just a **Booze Business** global executive; he's a "street smart" intellectual with a keen business sense. Above all, he's a terrific guy, and fun to work with.

Like most of us on the APU export business, Jett believed in the potential of Soyombo, particularly in the U.S. His vision for the export venture involved a line of Mongolian alcohol products, including a portfolio of vodkas at different price points, and Mongolian beer as well. Jett had what every company longs for in an expat executive— brains, commitment, and passion. He moved his family from Seattle to Ulan Bator.

Jett was initially effective. He had a clear vision as to how to market the country and the vodka. He overcame obstacles, opened markets, expanded operations—and in short, brought order and business discipline to a company that didn't have a clue.

In the U.S., with Jett and James' involvement, I set up a strong and comprehensive operation, overcame distributor reluctance to take on another vodka (particularly from a country they couldn't find on a map), and developed strong business and marketing plans.

By the summer of 2013, we had opened one Canadian and five U.S. markets. We began to get attention and some traction, in spite of the obstacles we faced from the APU management.

APU is the biggest alcohol and beverage company on the Mongolian Stock Exchange. In Mongolia, they are the dominant player in vodka and beer—at least in volume, and in my opinion, in terms of product quality too. The company was established in 1924 as a state monopoly (with Soviet influence), and in 1992 became a joint stock company; partly owned by the state, and partly private. Today it's a non-government company, registered on the Mongolian exchange.

The principal owner is erudite and charming, and he runs a wide range of companies in addition to APU. So many more companies, that he's pulled hither and yon and doesn't seem to focus or follow through as effectively as he should. Again, just in my opinion, he's one of those executives who is loyal to a fault, and hangs on to the managers who have succeeded in the past, even when they can no longer keep their heads above water. I also thought he was a bit fickle, often falling in and out of love with consultants, and others from outside the company and country. You know the type—whoever whispers in his ear last, wins the day.

The day-to-day running of the alcohol production company was left to a chief executive, in whose hands the export operation was also placed. The gentleman was a capable production guy, and has developed a top-notch manufacturing operation. But his lack of overall business acumen is only surpassed by his inability to comprehend the merits of an export business.

When I was at Seagram, we appreciated having a global enterprise; not only because of its overall contribution to the growth of the company, but also in a day-to-day sense. A down revenue year in the Americas, for example, could be offset by a strong year in Europe or Asia, or vice versa. That's not how this executive looked at the export operation.

The export business was not something he wanted, and it came with investments that cut into his profit responsibilities. As the pressure on the domestic business's revenue and profits grew, his annoyance/disdain for the export operation accelerated. Never mind that one day the export business could relieve downturn pressures—this executive could not see past his quarterly balance sheet.

But it was worse than that. The dislike and resentment of the export operation turned this otherwise affable person into a villain. Almost from the outset, he made Jett's life miserable; with tons of bureaucratic edicts, budget obstacles, and even reneging on commitments he'd made. It was a nightmare, as each and every plan or effort for the U.S. had to be reviewed, and was often turned down for capricious reasons. It was worst for Jett, who had to deal with the executive's anger on a daily basis.

In January of 2014, we were informed that the general export operation, and the U.S. in particular, needed to be cut back. Only two markets were allowed to continue, but only on a maintenance mode and budget. All other activity was to stop. Strike One.

Despite the traction we were getting, despite the favorable press, the Chairman decided to hire a consulting firm to review the export operation, with an eye towards improvement. What improvement, I wondered? If you leave us alone, we'll deliver faster than you expect. But that was not to be—they brought in one of those companies that specialize in taking your watch, in order to tell you the time. To the tune of a million dollar project. Strike Two.

To this day, I cannot understand why a company would spend that much money, while at the same time, cutting off the arms and legs of a promising business expansion.

The Mongolian economy weakened further; the government was pressed for revenue and raised taxes on businesses, payable only in hard currency. At the same time, the chickens (or should I say yaks) came home to roost, and the overleveraged other companies ran into financial difficulty. Strike Three.

In July of 2014, the APU Company had their 90-year celebration. While I missed the festivities, I was there for an intensive meeting with the consulting firm, the executive in charge, and his entourage. At the end of the meeting, we were informed that the financial situation was dire; the consulting firm needed to cease their work, and the export operation was shelved. The fat lady sang and the opera ended.

Lots of questions were left unanswered—but one thing was clear to me. Even a large company with deep pockets can easily lose the business development game. Fear of missed targets and loss of salary or bonus can far outweigh potential long-term benefits. Global expansion and business development is not for the faint of heart.

One positive thing I will say about the APU exit is how they did it with grace and care. The guiding principle was to manage the exit in a "correct and honorable" manner.

I was given six months to manage the dismantling of what could have been a major brand in the U.S. vodka market.

I suppose I will not be going to Mongolia again. But I will miss it.

*   *   *

India

India is the cradle of the human race, the birthplace of human speech, the mother of history, the grandmother of legend, and the great-grandmother of tradition. Our most valuable materials in the history of man are treasured up in India only!

- Mark Twain

Some time ago, Mr. Bishan Kumar contacted me; he is the group editor of Spiritz, an Indian magazine focusing on the liquor trade. Mr. Kumar is my type of editor/publisher—someone with a passion for his publication and his readers. We hit it off from the beginning, and next thing you know, I was writing a monthly column for his publication called "Booze Abroad."

It made me think about how little most Americans know about India. From an alcohol industry perspective, India is the subject of many misconceptions, and until recently, you could have included my own lack of knowledge in that criticism.

Their spirits business is the third largest in the world (250+ million cases), and ahead of the U.S., which is fourth. The industry is dominated by brown spirits, and growing at the rate of 18 to 20% per year.

The dominant factor in the market is Indian Made Foreign Liquor (IMFL), and all the major global players have a presence in the country. In fact, the #2 player is Pernod Ricard India Ltd., which had an 8% volume share of spirits in 2010. (By the way, that company was previously Seagram India Ltd. Enough said.)

The future outlook for spirits in India is quite good, based on a number of factors: rising income levels and a growing middle class, a youthful population, international travel, and exposure to premium products. All that is fueling a demand for imported products like tequila/mezcal and bourbon/other U.S. whiskies. Currently whisk(e)y, vodka, and rum dominate the market.

And it's not just about liquor. Beer is flying off the shelves there too, and the wine business, while still small, is growing.

All in all, it's a fascinating country with a robust booze industry. With all my international travel, I'm sorry to say I've never been to India—which is something I hope to change soon.

*   *   *

Update:

Since this post was written in 2011, India has become the second largest spirits-consuming country in the world, after China and before Russia. The U.S. is number 4. (Guess who is number 5? South Korea.)

*   *   *

The Columbian Exchange – Ever Heard of it?

One of the most important events in history.

The Columbian Exchange (sometimes called the Grand Exchange) was the exchange of goods and ideas from Europe, Africa, and Asia, with goods and ideas from the Americas. A historian named Alfred Crosby was said to have coined the phrase in 1972, describing the exchange of crops and livestock between the New World and the Old World.

The New World, for example, received such staples of our diet as citrus, apples, bananas, onions, coffee, wheat, and rice. In exchange, the Old World received such plants as maize, tomato, vanilla, cacao, and potato.

In terms of influence, consider this:

Before Columbus discovered the Americas, there were no potatoes in Ireland. By the 1840s, the Irish Potato Famine caused deaths and massive emigration. Tomatoes came to Spain from the New World, went from there to Italy, and forever changed the culinary style of the country.

As far as livestock is concerned, most of the exchange went from the Old World to the New World; including horses, pigs, cattle, chickens, large dogs, and cats. Not many animals went the other way, with the notable exception of the turkey. Oh, and let's not forget that when it comes to diseases, the Old World sent far more than it received—from measles to malaria.

What does this have to do with booze? Ah, glad you asked.

A reader of my blog named Desmond Nazareth, who lives in India, got in touch to tell me about his company—Agave India Industries Ltd. Turns out Mr. Nazareth is an entrepreneur, a graduate from the prestigious Indian Institute of Technology, Madras, and he is producing authentic artisanal spirit made from Agave Americana. If you look at the list of New World to Old World exchanges, the agave plant is right up there.

He can't call it tequila or even mescal, due to appellation requirements; but if it looks like a duck, walks like a duck, swims like a duck—you get the idea—it must be a duck.

*   *   *

Consider some "local" alcohol beverages that resulted directly from the Columbian Exchange:

- *Grape-based Pisco, with Chile contesting Peru for "ownership"*

- *Grape-based wines in California, Chile, Argentina, etc.*

- *Agave-based spirits in India*

- *Molasses and sugarcane-based rum and cachaça in the Caribbean and South America*

- *Single-malt whisky in Brazil, Japan, and many other countries*

- *Sweet potato using Soju in Korea and Shōchū in Japan*

*   *   *

Agave India: What's in a name?

A tequila product from India? Yes, that's right. But even though Agave India produces an outstanding 100% Agave product, the terms "tequila" or even "mezcal" are protected by designation of origin registration, and reserved for use by Mexico.

As a result, Agave India Industries Pvt Ltd., the craft distiller behind Agave India, can only use the generic Agave designation and have to be content with the following on their promotional material: "100% Agave product, a gift of the blue-green Agave plant. A plant grown in the red and black volcanic soils of India's Deccan plateau and nourished in a semi-arid micro-climate similar to that of Central America."

Undeterred by this, and secure in the knowledge that he makes world-class spirits products, Desmond Nazareth (under the brand name DesmondJi®) has been producing his products since 2011.

The term *Ji* is a suffix used in India as a sign of respect, also known as an honorific, and comparable to the Japanese *–san* or the Mexican *Don*, as in Don Julio. Kind of ironic, actually, since I couldn't tell the difference between DesmondJi 100% Agave and Don Julio Blanco in a blind taste test. Yes, it's that good.

Desmond moved to the U.S. as a software entrepreneur. In 2000, he returned to India. But while in the States, his bar at home became known among his friends as the place to go for the best margaritas. Alas, back in India, tequila products were not widely available (and still aren't, due to tariffs), much less orange liqueurs or margarita blends. Too bad, he thought.

But if you're an entrepreneur, a problem can easily become an opportunity.

Desmond spent several years researching agave plants and the making of agave spirits; he took trips to Mexico to study cultivation and distillation. Back in India, he recalled seeing the distinctive agave plant in the Deccan plateau. Consequently, he built a micro-distillery, and now produces a range of products. Agave India is the country's first fully integrated "field to bottle" alcohol beverage company, focusing on global spirits that are made to international standards, with Indian raw materials and know-how.

When Desmond and I spoke, I asked what the enormous agave plants were used for before he came along. He told me, "They were used as fences."

Under the DesmondJi label, the company produces a 100%, a 51% Agave spirit, and a 51% Agave Gold spirits with an oak finish. In addition to that, they have an Orange and Blue Curacao liqueur made with the Nagpur orange. After all, you can't make a decent margarita without an orange liqueur, and if you're using Indian agave, you should also use a liqueur made from Indian oranges. They produce alcoholic margarita blends—or as we call it, a premixed margarita.

Finally, his portfolio also contains a Pure Cane spirit (think cachaça) made from locally grown sugar cane.

While India is primarily a (scotch) whisky drinking country, white spirits like vodka and tequila have shown growth and future promise. But for now, at least, non-whisky alcohol products are a drop in the barrel—uh, bucket.

Desmond would like to set his sights on the U.S., the largest tequila-consuming market in the world. But I don't need to tell you that while not yet saturated, the U.S. tequila market is very cluttered. Can a craft agave spirit from India gain a foothold? Even if its terroir and geographic location is comparable to that of Mexico?

Still, the Indian population in the U.S. (according to the *Times of India*, March 22, 2012) is the third largest from Asia, after those from China and the Philippines. They are mainly centered in the Boston to D.C. megalopolis, and in Northern California. I've been told that more than 60% of retailers in New Jersey are from the Indian sub-continent, and in New York City it is roughly 45%.

So the question is—will consumers from India or who are of Indian ancestry have an interest in agave spirits from India? Will retailers?

Maybe it's not about national pride or appellation alone. Maybe it's about a high quality product that uses these two elements to kick-start a venture in the U.S.

To me, it's like brandy vs. cognac or champagne vs. prosecco—it's not about nomenclature, it's about quality.

Drinking in China

I came across an article from *The Guardian* with the headline "The Rise of Binge Drinking in China." The sub-headline was even more intriguing:

Binge drinking is increasingly common for Chinese professionals—often it's even in the job description.

We're not talking about people in the **Booze Business**, either.

It reminded me of my brief sojourn as head of marketing for Asia-Pacific/Global Duty Free.

The assignment was, as they say, both good news and bad news. On the one hand, it was my first head of marketing position, global in scope and in a new frontier—Asia. A dream come true. What's not to like?

Plenty. Spending two to three weeks per month away from home, and working for the mean-spirited gentleman I wrote about earlier.

Two strikes, but easily offset, at least initially, by the terrific people and the excitement of the new frontier. The drinking was another matter. Let's go back to the article:

Drinking to develop and cement relationships has a long history in China. "When one drinks with a friend, a thousand cups are not enough," runs one traditional saying.

I would not have put it so elegantly. When I was there, I feared the words Yam Sing, that literally meant, "Dry your cup" or "Bottoms up." Oh, how I hated those words!

The big push in China at the time was Martell Cognac, recently acquired by Seagram. The presence of Cognac in the portfolio, then and now, is important for business development in China. And man oh man; our people loved their Cognac. At dinners, we had Cognac as cocktails (straight) with dinner (no wine) and of course after dinner. Every glass was accompanied by those two dreaded words—*Yam Sing*. Someone would stand up, raise a glass, say some words in Mandarin or Cantonese, and end with the fearful phrase. It was bad face not to drain your glass/tumbler, even if it had been filled to the brim. No sniffing, no swirling, no gazing at the golden hues— just down the hatch.

Don't get me wrong; I like Cognac in small amounts, in a snifter, maybe by a fireplace on a cold winter night after an exceptional meal. Down the hatch or bottoms up are not the ways in which I enjoy it. After a few weeks of this, the migraines set in.

I asked my colleagues in the region the reason for the Cognac before and with meals. The answers were not helpful. They ranged from "strong food needs a strong drink," or "Cognac is very western and very masculine," and the all-time favorite (said with a wink of the eye) "excellent aphrodisiac." I would think in response to each reason: Chinese food is actually best with good beer; "western and macho" means cowboys and whiskey; what good is an aphrodisiac when you have a throbbing headache?

One day, the solution finally occurred to me.

At most dinners, I made it a point to sit near a potted plant, pretend to take a drink when no one was looking, and "down the hatch" was the plant's problem. Must have destroyed more plants than any disease had ever done. Hey, I'm not proud of it—but it was either a headache or the plant.

"FINALLY! WE HAVE CAUGHT THE PLANT KILLER."

International Assignment

Despite my less-than-positive experiences later on, as you've just read, I was initially very excited about the new job. I thought, "Wow, head of marketing for Asia-Pacific/ Global Duty Free; the wild west of the spirits business, destined to grow in importance."

First order of business: take the physical and get some shots.
So off I went to the medical office, where I had a visit to the company doctor and nurse. The Doc was pleasant enough, and I passed with flying colors.

The nurse was another story. Very competent, very capable, but dour... we're talking beyond focused, a combination of resolute and sour. On top of that, think of the Church Lady from Saturday Night Live. But she was well intentioned.

"Okay," she said to me, "You need shots before you can go to Asia."

"What kind of shots?" I asked. I'm not afraid of needles, but what the hell?

"Well, tetanus, malaria, a series of hepatitis, cholera, all sorts of disease preventatives."

"Is this really necessary?" I asked.

"Yes—you never can tell what you'll encounter...where you will be...what you'll be eating." Then, with a little glee in her voice, she added, "Besides, it's company policy."

Some time later, she finished administering the shots, and I got off the table, ready to leave.

"Just one more thing," she said. "Here's a Dopp kit that contains items you may need while traveling."

I looked inside to see a bizarre assortment of stuff: a pack of analgesics, Band-Aids, iodine, Alka Seltzer, and assorted travel-related items. Things I already traveled with.

But there, at the bottom of the kit, was a condom. I couldn't resist mentioning it.

I took it out and held it up. "What's this for?" I teased.

The nurse turned crimson, and said angrily, "You know full well what it's for."

"Yes," I answered, "But why only one?"

She stormed off. Good thing I got the shots first.

It Ain't Always Carnaval

When the music stopped during the never-ending corporate version of musical chairs, I found myself with the glorious (or was it to be inglorious?) title of Executive Vice President Marketing and Strategy, Seagram Americas.

From Canada to Chile, as I liked to say, I learned about the international side of the business, cultural differences, people, and working style differences. In fact, Canada was a dream. Despite the business and profitability constraints, the Canadian operation was top of the game.

South America was another matter.

The Americas were run by a South American ex-pat who was smart and hard working, but who was also a micromanager with an occasional reluctance to pull the trigger. In other words, he was tough to work for.

But all in all, the experience was terrific. Where else but Latin America are the following expressions a life principle?

It's better to apologize than ask permission.

A red traffic light is merely a suggestion.

All things are possible (said while rubbing the thumb, index, and middle fingers—the universal sign for money).

But then, and now even more so, security while traveling was an important issue. On one of the first trips, I was met by a driver/security person just outside of immigration, who chastised me for putting my passport into the breast pocket of my jacket. I was informed that I wouldn't get out of the building without having my pocket picked.

Big deal, I thought. A friend of mine had his wallet picked on the streets of Paris.

Then I heard about a French colleague who was mugged during daylight in Sao Paulo. Another had his computer ripped out of his hands in Mexico City. Most of my South American associates lived in gated communities, but unlike the U.S., the gatekeepers had machine guns.

So what? I thought. I grew up in Brownsville, Brooklyn, and the world is a tough place.

Then one fine day I got a wake up call.

The Swedish partners (Absolut) decided to concentrate on expanding the business in Latin America, and wanted to have a conference to discuss brand development issues in the continent. Their marketing people wanted the meeting to be held in Bogota, Colombia. I wasn't pleased, but whatever... never been there, how bad could it be?

To go there, I needed a visa, and had to go through Corporate to get things arranged. That's where the story begins.

I came into my office one day, and my assistant Mary Mastrianni says, "You can't go to Bogota because Leo won't let you."

The scene shifts to Leo McGillicudy—the nicest and most decent person I had met at the company. Head of security and a former FBI agent, Leo was a friend and someone I respected and admired.

"What the hell? I'll call him," I said to Mary, knowing full well that if Leo said no, it was no.

Me: "Hi Leo. How's the family?" (Pause) "Great...listen Leo, what's this about my not being able to go to Bogota?"

Leo: "Are you nuts? Do you read the papers? It isn't safe, and I can't let you go."

Me: "Come on, it's my job, how bad can it be?"

Leo: "Are you listening? The last thing I need at this point in my life is to have to go to Bogota and save your sorry ass."

Me: "What am I am suppose to tell my boss?"

Leo: "Whatever you want. You aren't going."

Me: "But he's from Latin America, and I'm new on his staff...what's he going to think when I tell him I'm not going?"

Leo: "I don't give a shit. Tell him I said he can't go either."

The meeting was held in Aruba.

Note: On a recent trip through the Panama Canal, we docked at Cartagena, and I thought it was a wonderful city, charming and safe.

Ireland

After a holiday in the Emerald Isle, here are some thoughts about my favorite topic—Jameson.

Seagram had the distribution rights to this Irish whiskey for quite some time, and frankly, didn't do much with it. With the exception of St. Patrick's Day promotions and pushing the Irish Coffee drink, the brand went nowhere for years. I suppose it's understandable; with millions of scotch sales at the heart of the portfolio, there was little room for this great brand.

Irish Distillers took the brand back, and a series of smart moves set Jameson on a growth path under the leadership of Richard Burrows, a very smart industry executive. The Irish Distillers Group controlled all the major brands of whiskey, and consolidated the production and marketing. In other words, they focused their efforts. Ultimately, Pernod Ricard took over the company.

Today, the brand is one of the fastest growing in the U.S. spirits industry, with annual growth rates in the 20-25% range. There are lots of factors at play contributing to its success; including Pernod's focus, consumer interest in its unique taste and strong imagery, shot usage, interesting drinks, and more recently, the advertising.

Bushmills, the other major Irish whiskey recently acquired by Proximo Spirits, has also grown steadily—but pales in comparison to Jameson. It doesn't seem to have the same attributes among consumers. Let's not forget that Bushmills is also from Northern Ireland (U.K.), while Jameson is made in the Republic of Ireland, in the south.

I find it fascinating to consider these booze brands and Irish history. Ireland became independent in 1922; prior to that it was a country occupied and ruled by the Vikings, the Normans, and for 800 years, the British.

Today, the national whiskey brands come from either the French or the British. In fact, in Ireland, roughly 3 million cases of all spirits are sold each year with Diageo (30%) and Pernod (35%) being the dominant players.

For my ex-Seagram friends:

My wife and I visited the Cliffs of Moher. This is a world-renowned landmark towering above the Atlantic by over 700 feet, with breathtaking views. That is—when it's not shrouded in mist and fog, as was the case when we were there.

Every now and then, a gust of wind would blow, and for a few brief moments you could catch a glimpse of the magnificent views; only to have the visibility blocked again moments later.

My wife, a veteran of many Seagram trips and over-the-top efforts to accommodate executives and distributors, remarked, "If this were a Seagram trip, there would be giant fans all over the place to keep the mist and fog away."

No question about it.

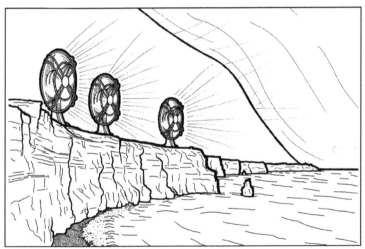

COURTESY OF SEAGRAM

11. Breaking the Ban on TV Advertising in the U.S.—I hear you knocking, but you can't come in

A friend and I were watching a sports event on TV, and he looked at me in surprise when a liquor ad came on. "Hey, wait a minute," he said, "I thought it was against the law for liquor to advertise on TV."

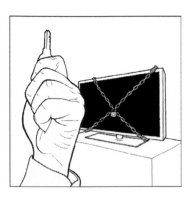

My answer: it was never against the law. The ban on radio and television advertising for spirits (liquor) was voluntary and self-imposed by the industry. In the mid-1990s, as head of marketing for the U.S. at Seagram Spirits and Wine, among my responsibilities and accomplishments was breaking the ban.

The restrictions today are also voluntary, but limited to after 10:00 p.m. for TV, and content depending for radio. Above all, the broadcast medium outlet audience composition must be at least 71.6% over legal drinking age, which is 21 years of age throughout the U.S.

In my view, any restrictions—voluntary or imposed—on liquor remain hypercritical, because wine and beer (mainly) do not face comparable constraints in the U.S.

But that, my friends, is the story.

The history behind the ban

When Prohibition in the U.S. ended, distillers got together and agreed upon further standards and practices to avoid a reoccurrence of that event. Between the do's and don'ts, they voluntarily decided to ban radio advertising. When television came along, the self-imposed ban applied to that medium, as well.

Meanwhile, the wine and beer people did not feel the need to follow suit—nor did they want to.

Over the next 50 to 60 years, people began to believe that 1) the ban was a law and 2) spirits were characterized as "hard," while wine and beer were not.

By the mid-90s, this legacy had hurt spirits in a number of ways. From a marketing standpoint, access to important brand building media was denied. More painfully, the hard vs. soft perception led to a lack of equivalency among alcohol types, particularly in the area of federal excise taxes, with liquor being taxed the most. The lack of equivalency was also an issue among consumers, regarding what type of alcohol to drink and when.

When one of my daughters was attending her high school prom, I asked the father of the boy who was driving whether he and his son had discussed drinking and driving; and whether he was confident that Johnny would follow the rules. The father assured me all would be well; he had given Johnny a 6-pack, to be sure he stayed away from the "hard" stuff. The follow-up conversation was less than pleasant, but it made me realize how confused the public was on the issue.

Seagram fought the tax equivalency problem in a number of ways. The most important was promoting the idea that *a drink is a drink*, and 1.5 oz. of spirits is equivalent to 12 oz. of beer and 5 oz. of wine. Despite the accuracy and acceptance by experts of this claim, it wasn't easy to get the message across. Even print media was reluctant to run ads containing this concept.

Another effort aimed at TV involved the introduction of Seagram mixers. While it got the name across, the benefits were limited to those brands carrying the name, and it addressed the equivalency issue only in part. Besides, it was a back door approach to changing consumer and government perceptions. "How can you claim to be equivalent when they (wine and beer) are on TV and you're not? You're more than alcohol, you're hard liquor." The public affairs people wanted more direct efforts to change the situation.

Enter marketing

Usually, marketing and public affairs people aren't on the same page. In this case, ending the voluntary ban was a strong second item on their respective agendas—more than enough for an alliance.

The situation was complicated. The Seagram advertising budget could not sustain a full-scale foray into broadcast advertising. In fact, total liquor industry advertising spending was a fraction of just one of the major beer companies.

From a brand-building standpoint, I really didn't care about national TV. I had no dreams about or interest in sponsoring the Super Bowl or some other mega event. Beer marketing is based on mass appeal and efforts; spirits marketing is about reaching the correct (albeit smaller) audience effectively. That meant our ultimate efforts needed to center on local or cable TV and spot radio.

The only way to accomplish these objectives was to swing for the fences, and go for an end to the voluntary ban.

The challenges

The first order of business was to approach other spirits manufacturers informally, through DISCUS (Distilled Spirits Council of the U.S.). None of these manufacturers were initially ready or willing to step up to the plate. Thanks to the clout the public affairs executive had with the Seagram family and management, it was decided that we would do it alone.

Interestingly, not everyone in management was in love with the idea of adding radio and TV to the spending mix. There were lots of reasons: fear of change, concern about increased spending, and my personal favorite, "how do we know it will benefit our brands?" Duh. Now we had a two-front war, breaking the ban and making dozens of presentations to show that broadcast advertising works. Ah, the power of fear of change.

Given the go ahead, the strategy was simple. It was called the "crawl strategy;" as in, we will slowly and quietly crawl into broadcast. No fanfare, no hoopla, no press conference, just do it—buy the space and slowly expand from market to market before anyone notices, and by the time they do, it will have been a fait accompli.

Ha! When we started to crawl, we must have been wearing noisemakers, because the country heard us the very next day following the initial effort.

Will you take our ads?

Objectives, plans, authorization, and strategy in place, we needed a partner—a broadcast media company or station that would run our ads. Our ads, by the way, were entertaining and humorous, very tasteful, and effectively got our message across in a low-key manner.

Finding a media partner was extremely difficult. The explicit reason given was "I love the idea, and could use the new source of revenue, but I don't want to be the first to break the voluntary ban... come see me after someone else breaks the ice." Such courage. But who can blame them? In the game of "follow the money," there was not enough for them to justify the risk.

Additionally, I suspect there was a deep fear of losing beer revenue or being otherwise punished, if they accepted our ads and helped to break the ban. A few media executives told me privately about threats of losing beer advertising if our ads were taken. But all that managed to do was embolden us further.

In the midst of the battle, I received a phone call from one of our Texas distributors, Phil Boeck. He knew of a small local TV station (KRIS-TV Channel 6, an affiliate of NBC in Corpus Christi Texas) that wanted liquor ads on their station. The station owner, T. Frank Smith Jr., despite the fact that his audience was overwhelmingly comprised of teetotalers, wanted our ads to run. Maybe it was the potential revenue, perhaps it was his sense of fairness and the belief that alcohol is alcohol, possibly it was his belief in free speech, whatever... we were on the air in June 1996.

On the air

The brand we had chosen to break the voluntary ban was Crown Royal, a premium Canadian whiskey with a strong following in the South and especially Texas. The crown jewel in our portfolio, the brand had a long pedigree and was known for its understated, clever, wry humor.

The ad we developed for TV followed this same style. It showed two dogs (elegant Weimaraners) graduating from dog obedience school. One dog came out holding a diploma in its mouth, and the voiceover said, "obedience school graduate." The other entered holding a bottle of Crown Royal whiskey by the drawstrings of the purple bag. In this case, the voiceover said, "valedictorian." Throughout the ad, the background music was "Pomp and Circumstance."

The ad ran over a weekend in June 1996, and the reaction far exceeded my expectations. It made the front page of newspapers, and the TV news people had a field day with the story. I gave dozens of interviews, and had more than my "15 minutes of fame." So much for the "crawl-on-the-air" strategy.

OBEDIENCE SCHOOL GRADUATE.   VALEDICTORIAN.

There was a recap of events by the Center for Science in the Public Interest (CSPI). (CSPI is a well-known anti-alcohol group.)

June 1996 -- Seagram airs an ad for Crown Royal Canadian Whiskey on KRIS-TV, an NBC affiliate in Corpus Christi, Texas, breaking a long-standing, voluntary industry ban on broadcast liquor ads. The ban had been in effect for 60 years on radio (since 1936) and 48 years (since 1948) on television. Local and national groups protest; Rep. Kennedy and more than a dozen co-sponsors introduce the "Just Say No Act" (HR 3644) to ban liquor ads on radio and television to maintain status quo. President Clinton (in a Saturday radio address) asks industry to go back to the ban.

Sure enough, I was informed that President Clinton, in his Father's Day address to the nation, was going to call for the liquor industry to revert back to the ban. Recognizing this as a political move in an election year—and considering the financial and other support Seagram had given the President—management decided to stay the course and continue to run the ads. Ignoring the President is in the province of the very rich or very stupid.

I was also informed that a TV network would interview me, so I could tell our side of the story, and in effect, offer a rebuttal. What? I'm supposed to disagree with the President on national TV. Are you kidding me? No way I come out of this looking anything less than a fool.

The PR people and I decided that if we were going to do this—and we had no other choice, management was adamant—then I would stick to a carefully worded script and not deviate one iota. To the chagrin of the interviewer, I had four things to say, and no matter what I was asked, I stuck to those responses. After a while, the interviewer gave up, the piece was cut short, and my rambling stayed the course of the main issues— alcohol is alcohol; why wine and beer are allowed but not liquor; how the ban was voluntary and right for its time; and something about freedom of speech. No counterattack on Clinton, no overt disagreement, no ranting and raving, just the facts and our story. It made for a poor rebuttal interview, but avoiding a confrontation was a good career move.

One of the lessons I learned is that the broadcast news media want a story at any price, the more provocative the better. Without media training and preparation, one can easily allow good judgment to succumb to the spotlight and the ego. In other words, be careful not to step on any portion of your own anatomy.

The aftermath

There was, and still is, a happy ending. At Seagram, we not only stayed the course, but also expanded our TV efforts to three different Crown Royal advertising executions, and ran them through local affiliates of the networks and on cable. More brands were added to the mix. The initial objective of radio advertising that was tied into promotional activity was met and exceeded.

As for the brand itself, the news coverage and press about the TV ads resulted in incredible double-digit growth for Crown Royal. As the coverage unfolded, wherever the story ran, the ad was shown. In effect, we paid a fraction for the amount of coverage and exposure we received. Not the intent of the effort—but a nice dividend.

The anti-alcohol forces continued to shout about our sinfulness, but to no avail. One group even went so far as to accuse us of deliberately attempting to subvert American youth into the perils of demon rum via the dogs and graduation. In their view, the dog with a bottle of booze was valedictorian, and this was our attempt to show how drinking leads to success! Give me a break.

The other spirits companies who avoided participation at the outset not only jumped on the bandwagon, but a few claimed the effort as their own idea. Success has many parents.

Even the doubters among my management became believers, and broadcast advertising became a focal point of national and regional brand building efforts.

Today, after 10:00 p.m. on some content appropriate television programs, it is not unusual to see liquor ads. Lots of them. This includes national network TV.

But please, don't ask me to assess the quality of the ads. That's a whole other matter.

*   *   *

An interesting side story: Beware the media buyers...

While I never worked as a media buyer, throughout my career I've had many occasions to work with and manage the people responsible for placing advertising in publications and on the air. In effect, these are the folks who work for ad agencies or media buying companies, and negotiate the rates.

Too often these buyers are myopic, and push for formulas that do not take into account the quality of the audience reached or sensible business practice. While this may have changed, and perhaps doesn't apply all over the world, I have found that some, but not all media buyers tend to be enslaved by the cost per thousands (CPM) and lose sight of the forest for the trees.

At Seagram, we had our own in-house media buying department. But when it came to the break-the-ban wars, they were either missing in action or got in the way.

As our efforts to get on the air progressed, we had many defeats ("I can't run your ads now, but maybe at a later time"), and a few cherished victories. Breaking the ban was not enough; we needed a sustained presence on television.

Among our allies was a cable network called The Golf Channel. This was perfect for us—no issues with underage drinkers, and the audience was older, affluent, sophisticated, and all premium quality drinkers. It was an ideal setting for Chivas Regal and The Glenlivet. We even sponsored a program on golf tips.

One day, the owner of the media company called and hesitantly asked to see me.

This could only mean a problem, since the usual approach was to go through the media department.

After exchanging pleasantries, I could see that the gentleman was agitated, and it didn't take long for him to blurt it out. Our esteemed media department had cut The Golf Channel from the new budget. Considering they were the second or third station to take our ads, I was partly perplexed, and partly very angry.

On the spot, I called one of the buyers and asked about it. "I understand that we've cut The Golf Channel from the plans," I politely asked. "How come?"

"Well," came the reply, "they are too expensive."

"What are you talking about?" I asked.

"Their CPM is twice as high as XYZ channel."

"Tell me," I asked, "does XYZ take our advertising?"

"No, they don't," was the answer.

"So if I got this straight...we are dropping one of the few channels who will take our ads because their cost per thousand is higher than a channel which will not take our ads. Is that correct?"

He said, rather sheepishly, "I didn't look at it that way...just compared costs."

They were put back on the schedule immediately.

12. The Craft Revolution—It's what's in the bottle that matters

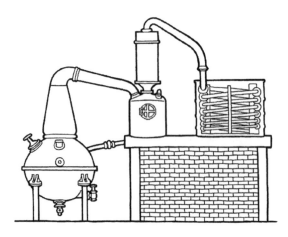

This is a time of change for the alcohol industry; and the change is coming from the drinking public, not the industry.

In beer and liquor particularly, quality of drinking has replaced quantity. While there are still pockets of "resistance," the mainstream consumer is more concerned with how these products are made and how best to consume them, rather than how to get plastered. Borrowing a page from the wine industry, beer and liquor are going through a sort of "vinification," whereby ingredients, process, water, and even terroir are important considerations. And, mixologist and bar chefs are moving the bartender craft to new levels and new experiences for consumers.

It's not a pleasant time for the Big Boys (mainstream companies) struggling to adapt. Some are in denial; some think they can ridicule it (as in ads by Budweiser) some are buying their way in; and some are moving into the craft direction, in both fact and fiction.

Let's look at some at some postings and stories about the craft movement.

*   *   *

Craft Confusion

When is the term "craft" authentic and when is it marketing hype?

The spirits industry has seen an amazing growth of craft distillers and brands. The Distilled Spirits Council of the U.S. (DISCUS) has reported that there were nearly 800 "small" distilleries producing 3.5 million cases in 2014 (up from 700,000 in 2010), with revenues of nearly half a billion dollars.

This craft spirits development is here to stay, based on a number of factors. These factors include the interest in whiskies of all types; consumer trends regarding connoisseurship, craftsmanship and general artisanal products; the focus on ingredients, process, and the distiller; and attention to what's in the bottle.

There are other forces at play here, particularly the rejection of mass-produced products in favor of small batches and handcrafted; a phenomenon affecting all consumer businesses from packaged goods to durables.

So it's not surprising that the power of the words "craft," "handmade," and "small batch" would be adopted and used by large brands, despite the intent of these words. When a brand sells hundreds of thousands or millions of cases, one needs to wonder whether the use of these words is marketing hype (as in "smooth"), or outright fraud. At the same time, there are also small distillers jumping on the bandwagon without the real credentials.

The lawsuits

The best and most succinct coverage of the debate and confusion can be found in the Feb 16, 2015 edition of *Wine & Spirits Daily*, under the headline "Truth Squad Discusses Transparency in Labeling Lawsuits." The "Truth Squad" is a panel of WSD readers (manufacturers and wholesalers) who express their professional views on a range of issues affecting the wine and spirits businesses.

There are a number of cases involving court action related to labeling:

- Templeton Rye was sued for claiming it was made in Templeton, Iowa, when it's in fact made in a large multi-brand distillery. The implication was that the brand was a small batch product. They have since revised their label.

- Tito's Vodka is being sued in California and Florida for the label claim that it's handmade, as in Tito's Handmade Vodka. At roughly a million cases, how can you call yourself handmade?

- Maker's Mark is also being sued for claims related to "handmade." According to USA Today, "The lawsuit...accused the distillery of deceptive advertising and business practices with its "handmade" promotion on the labels of its bottles, known for their distinctive red-wax seal." I know that they hand dip each bottle in the wax, but can you really hand make 1.3 million cases?

Don't get me wrong... I think these are outstanding, well-made products. I'm a fan of each of them, but the words in question are not marketing hype words like "smooth" or "premium." For many people, the misuse of these words is deceitful.

Enter the Truth Squad

One member thinks too much is being made of this issue, and suggests that the consumer doesn't know or care. Maybe. But how about the genuine small batch or craft distiller who has invested their life savings in a distillery, and whose livelihood depends on it?

Another view was that the lawyers "who make a fortune" with spurious lawsuits are behind it all. Perhaps. People who are looking for the real deal deserve not to be cheated with misleading claims. If the regulatory people won't deal with it, then the courts should.

A distributor executive put it nicely when he/she said in the same *WSD* article:

> I think that the average consumer feels better about purchasing something with the perceived or real support to a small company, and dislike it when they find out it's just part of a huge corporation. It would be... like someone buying... produce at a big box store, and then taking it to the Farmer's Market on a Saturday wearing overalls, and making money on the perception that they are a farmer.

What's the answer?

Simply put, there should be a standard by which those using the word "craft" (and related phrases) are held accountable. Don't expect the alcohol governing body (TTB, the Alcohol and Tobacco Tax and Trade Bureau) to do it. Even if they were so inclined, they don't have the resources to police these types of label claims. For the same reasons, forget about the Federal Trade Commission.

I think the craft distillers associations like American Distilling Institute, or American Craft Spirits Association, are trying to deal with the issue. The challenge they face is defining the term craft and certifying its use.

The shift that is occurring in the beer and spirits industries—called craft and/or handmade and/or small batch—is here to stay. Large manufacturers have lots of options for how to deal with this growing consumer interest. They can ignore it, and present the merits of their brands as is. They can attack it, like Budweiser's advertising. Or they can buy legitimate craft-made brands, and then screw it up—again, like Budweiser. But to co-opt or misuse these terms is just plain wrong.

I prefer the industry to clean its own house; but until then, I guess we'll continue to make the lawyers rich.

*   *   *

Update:

As of May 2015, the lawsuit against Maker's Mark was dismissed. The Judge ruled that "no reasonable person" would think the handmade claim is literal. But the suit against Tito's continues, as of this writing.

*   *   *

FEW Spirits: Contradictions Result in Excellence

Few Spirits, run by Paul Hletko in the Chicago suburb of Evanston, is based on a number of inconsistencies. He built a distillery in a town where prohibition ended in 1972 (40 years late), and where there is not a single bar, to this day. Furthermore, Evanston was the home of the Women's Christian Temperance Union, one of the driving forces behind the "noble experiment."

Oddly enough, the co-founder and longtime leader of the WCTU was Frances Elizabeth Willard, whose initial are F.E.W.

I asked Paul if he named the distillery and brands after her. His response was no. He named it Few as in selective, as in small, as in a few products.

Whatever the reason, he makes outstanding spirits.

Before I tell you about the products, let's spend a minute on Paul Hletko, who is not your typical startup distiller. According to Paul, "All my life, I've tried to be a creative person."

He has an engineering degree from Michigan, and is also an attorney. Prior to founding Few, Paul had a career in music; with a rock n' roll band, a record label, and a company focused on designing and building custom guitar effects pedals. None of that worked out.

This led his creative efforts to follow in the footsteps of his grandfather, who owned a brewery in Europe before World War II. But instead of beer, he decided to become a distiller, producing true farm-to-bottle products.

While many so-called craft distillers source their alcohol from industrial distilleries, Few is all about local ingredients; all grain used in his products (corn, wheat, rye, and barley) comes from within 100 miles (often closer) of his distillery.

In whiskies, Few produces a bourbon, a rye (outstanding), and a single malt. All are exceptional products.

But get this—Few makes three different style gins, including Few American Gin, essentially an American genever with 11 botanicals; Few Barrel Gin, a gin aged in new and used bourbon and rye barrels; and Few Standard Issue Gin, a gin that harkens back to traditional British navy gin at 114-proof.

I've sampled them all and this is what craft distillation is all about.

Aside from production issues, independent craft distillers face three tough hurdles: marketing, distribution, and financial resources. Few Spirits seems to be handling them well.

Take marketing, for example. In my experience, spirits startup entrepreneurs tend to be so in love with the chemistry, alchemy, and their skills and recipes, they often neglect a focus on marketing and sales. I've written about some exceptions—Jackie Summers and Sorel Liqueur, Alison Patel and Brenne Whisky—so add Paul Hletko to the group. From concept to packaging to promotion, PR, social media, etc., Paul knows what he's doing.

Distribution is another obstacle. The large mainstream wholesalers will either not want to talk to you, try to become your partner, expect you to buy your way in, or worst of all, take you in and let your brand gather dust. So Paul has put together a "hodge-podge" distribution network that includes Blueprint Brands, a division of Great Brewers, craft beer distributors. From what I can tell, his potpourri of wholesalers seems to be working out.

As for financial resources, well, that's none of my business. But from the look and feel of Few Spirits, and its approach to brand building, I'd say they're here for the long run.

Maybe he'll change the name from Few to Many.

Koval Distillery: Black Sheep of Booze

Chicago's first distillery since the mid-1800s.

The word Koval means "blacksmith" in many Eastern European languages. In Yiddish, the word also refers to a "black sheep," or someone "who forges ahead"...or someone who does things that are out of the ordinary.

I cannot think of a better description for the company founded in 2008 by husband and wife Robert and Sonat Birnecker. Both came to Chicago from Washington D.C., giving up successful careers to start a family-owned business that paid homage to their grandfathers. One was considered a black sheep of his family for leaving Austria to become a Chicago businessman; and the other was a distiller whose last name was Schmidt, which is German for Smith, as in blacksmith.

That grandfather, by the way, was the person who taught Robert the art of distillation.

But, Koval Distillery is more than just a craft distiller. Much more.

Let's start with Robert Birnecker's background. He's a fourth generation distiller, whose family still runs a distillery and winery in Austria. You can safely say that he combines traditional techniques with contemporary equipment.

This is a true craft distillery, making grain to bottle products. The grain is certified organic and sourced from the Midwest Organic Farmers Cooperative. The water is from Lake Michigan, using a natural charcoal purification method. All the enzymes and yeast are also organic. To top it off, their products are certified Kosher by the oldest and most trusted certification body.

Unlike some other distillers, who purchase or bottle premade spirits, Koval makes its organic spirits from scratch, using only the "heart" cut of the distillate for a cleaner whiskey taste. All of the whiskies are single barrel and aged in 30 gallon, charred barrels. In fact, each of the bottles identifies the barrel number from which it came. They control every step of the production process.

So far I've tasted three of their whiskies: Bourbon, Four Grain, and Rye. Sensational. The mash bill of the Four Grain is oat, malted barley, rye, and wheat; it's smooth as silk. The Bourbon is aged less than four years, and tasted smoother to me than products that are twice as old. Most of all, I loved the Rye whiskey.

When I interviewed Sonat Birnecker, I told her how much I liked the rye and how different it tasted from most ryes I've had. She called my attention to the back label, which indicates that the product contains 100% rye. Many ryes on the market are 51% (which is the minimum amount necessary to be called rye whiskey), plus other ingredients (usually corn or malted barley).

What you see and read on their label is what you get. No coloring, no added ingredients, no neutral grain spirits—nothing but what you are paying for.

By the way, their Rye Whiskey was awarded first place for Best International Whisky at Europe's 2013 InterWhisky Competition.
I have not yet met Robert Birnecker; but from what I've heard and read, he is a distiller's distiller.

I found this about him in the *Chicago Sun-Times*:

The Birneckers are the stateside and English-speaking representatives of Kothe, the German still-maker responsible for the copper behemoth eating up their warehouse space. With that job, the couple's workshops and their craft-distilling consulting business, Sonat estimates that the pair have advised one-third of the craft distillers that have opened in the U.S. and Canada in the past five years.

That's right—in addition to running Koval, Robert and Sonat consult and teach distillation. Robert is also a key lecturer at the Siebel Institute in Chicago. Among the distilleries he has helped set up, stills include Journeyman Distillery in Michigan and Few Spirits in Illinois. These are top of the game craft distillers.

In addition to the three whiskies I mentioned earlier, Koval also makes Oat and White Rye products. Interestingly, they produce a whiskey I haven't heard of before: Millet Whiskey, described on their website, "Millet is a prized grain in Asia and Africa and popular base for spirits in Nepal, though this is the first whiskey to be made out of millet." Definitely on my "must try" list.

There is also Koval Dry Gin, which my friends in Chicago think is the best on the planet. Here's how Koval describes it... "Made with a unique variety of woodland spices... Juniper and wildflowers envelop the nose, while the taste is dry, yet vibrant— clean and nuanced by emerald grasses, golden citrus, and white pepper with a round, floral body."

Finally, there is a line of seven liqueurs ranging from the expected (coffee, ginger) to the exotic (orange blossom, rose hip, chrysanthemum and honey, caraway, jasmine).

When it comes to marketing—and at the risk of offending my craft distiller friends—most craft distillers are outstanding at production, but very few seem to realize there is a consumer at the other end of the bottle. Koval gets it.

Koval's labeling, or should I say award-winning package design, speaks to the product and its craft/artisanal composition. As I mentioned, the label tells you which barrel it came from, and what it's distilled from.

They understand consumers and how to break out of the clutter, with excellent PR and very highly praised distillery tours. Koval even has a barrel program in which you select the barrels, and it is customized to a store, bar, restaurant, or even an individual. (Unfortunately, you have to buy the 25 to 30 cases that comprise the barrel. I'm saving up for it. Maybe a Kickstarter campaign?)

Their products are also available internationally, in Europe and Japan. In sum, Koval Distillery is a company in the finest tradition of the spirits industry. A company where they care about what they produce, and how they produce it... where tradition and heritage are embraced and built upon... where state-of-the-art is not marketing hype. Above all, this is a company that's here for the long run, and building for the future.

There aren't many like them these days.

Is There a Bubble in your Craft Beer?

Will the growth of craft breweries continue? Or will the bubble burst? There's been a lot of back-and-forth in the press (Time, USA Today, Beer Business Daily) over whether the craft beer industry is here to stay, or if the bubble will burst.

Bubble? Craft beer is here to stay.

According to the Brewers Association, the number of breweries at the end of 2013 reached over 2,700, the highest level since the 1870s. Despite the growth, American craft brewers account for only 9% of the beer category in the U.S. But craft beer production was up 9.6% in 2013, while overall beer production fell 1.4%, according to CNBC as reported by Buffalo Trace Newsletter.

According to the Brewer's Association, "an American craft brewer is small, independent and traditional." They provide some definitions related to craft brewers, such as: small brewers, emphasis on innovation, and the use of traditional ingredients, among other things.

I've got a better definition: craft beers are more flavorful, with more unique styles and brands—and they just taste better than mainstream beers.

Even the big boys see the "beer handwriting on the wall," and have been getting the craft game with what can only be called "crafty" beers, according to a recent article in Time. Check out these brands and who owns them: Blue Point, Goose Island, Shock Top, Red Hood (AB-Inbev), Blue Moon, Leinenkugel, and Killian's Irish Red (Miller Coors).

Among the definitions of a craft beer, mentioned above, is size. And in this case, size matters—a brewer must be independent, which means that less than 25% of the craft brewery is owned or controlled by an alcohol industry member, who is not themselves a craft brewer. In other words, a wolf in sheep's clothing can't be a craft brewer member of the Brewers Association. But it can be crafty.

What are the market segments of craft breweries? Here's where it gets interesting. Half (50%) of the craft breweries in the U.S. are microbreweries, and another 44% are brewpubs. So in effect, and by definition, the vast majority of craft brewers are small businesses, akin to Mom and Pop operations.

But they are much more than that. They are entrepreneurs with a passion for making quality, flavorful beer without the restrictions that large organizations impose. They understand how to meet the needs of changing taste preferences among consumers. In fact, a recent article in *Beer Business Daily* had this as a headline in their Nov 13, 2013 edition: "Wine and Craft Beer now in Direct Competition." It's based on a report by a consulting firm that compares craft beer to wine.

The study reported by *Beer Business Daily* suggests continued growth for craft beers based on: "shifting demographics (the rise of the Millennials), consumers' desire for quality, diversity and authenticity as well as unprecedented innovation in brewing, marketing and packaging." They further predict that the craft beer market will double, since we are still in the early days in the "premiumisation" of beer.

Hey, what about all those brewpubs that comprise the craft beer market—won't many of them fail? I suppose many will, but I also suppose that there will be others to take their place. According to *Business Insider*, the majority of New York restaurant startups fail in five years. Does that mean that the restaurant "bubble" will burst?

Finally, Bart Watson, economist at the Brewers Association, wrote an interesting article that gets at the heart of the so-called bubble issue. His central argument, in my view, is that craft beers at roughly 10% of beer consumption have a long way to go. That is, of course, so long as consumers continue to favor full-flavored beers over light lagers. I don't know about you, but I'm on board for the long run.

Remember earlier, when I mentioned the inroads into craft by the big multinational brewers? Here is what Bart has to say on the subject: "The fact that global players are diversifying into their own full-flavored product lines and investing in or buying up regional brewers proves the solidity of the consumer base on which craft sits."

So far as I can tell, the only bubble in craft beer is in the glass.

*　　*　　*

Updates:

From CNNMoney, *May 2015:*

> *Craft brewers now account for 11% of beer sales in the U.S., up from 6% just two years ago. In the U.K., analysts estimate craft beers have 10% of the market.*

From Wine and Spirits Daily, *July 2015:*

> *The U.S. craft spirits category is still small, but it's growing at a rapid pace (+58% in 2014). In fact, it could get ahold of as much as 8% volume share of the market by 2020, per a recent report from Exane BNP...*

From Grub Street, *October 2015:*

> *"In the last few years, its become clear that the independent brewers are winning: In 2012 there were 2,538 breweries in the United States. Now there are more than 3,700. That's an average of roughly two new breweries opening every day. Sales of megabrands like Bud Light and Miller are flat; craft beer, meanwhile, now accounts for 11 percent of all beer consumed in the U.S."*

The response from Big Beer:

From The Motley Fool, *October 2015:*

> *The beer battle for shelf space is under regulatory scrutiny as the Department of Justice reviews Anheuser-Busch InBev's distributor acquisitions over fears it may wield too much power... Following Prohibition, the government imposed a three-tiered system on the industry requiring brewers to sell their beer to a middle man, the distributors and wholesalers, which in turn sell to retailers, whether they're package good stores, bars, or grocery stores. The idea was to prevent the brewers from owning the retail operations and limiting consumer choice while hiking prices. But regulators have a poor ability to foresee the future, and now craft brewers are placed at a competitive disadvantage as the mass brewers buy up the distributors and crowd out the competition.*

*   *   *

The challenges faced by craft startups are more than just money and resources. These startups need to move beyond the production focus, and concentrate on sales and marketing. In this chapter, you've met a few people who understand it's the trade and consumers that make it happen. Those that have a broader view will survive, and the others will probably not.

But that focus is within their control. The narrowing of the distribution channel (distributors and wholesalers) is an unpleasant development. Consolidation and mergers, either as necessities or as forced by mega brands, are difficult and dangerous wild cards for these startup ventures.

13. Parting Shots—Cheers

I thoroughly enjoy writing about the alcohol industry. So permit me to share some of my favorite posts from over the years.

"Bartender, I'd like a hummer."

What's in a name?

A clever, memorable call name for a drink is what makes that drink popular. Where would Seagram's Seven be without a 7 and 7, or Peach Schnapps without the Fuzzy Navel?

Here's one for the books.

Four middle-aged women are out for their every-other-week ladies night out. They are feeling a bit adventurous this particular evening, and are chatting about what to have when the server walks up to their table.

Let's listen in:

Server: Hi ladies. Can I offer you something to drink?

Lady #1: A glass of chardonnay would be nice.

Lady # 2: (To the group) You know what, girls? I'm going to have a chocolate martini. I'm in that kind of mood.

Lady #1: Great idea... please change my drink to that.

Lady #3: Do you have any of that RumChata?

Server: No, I'm afraid not.

Lady #3: Then I'll just have Sex On the Beach.

(They all laugh. The server smiles.)

Server: Perfect choice for a cold winter night in Detroit. And you, ma'am?

Lady #4: I want a hummer.

All: A what?

Lady #4: What's the matter? My friend Louise says her husband begs her for a hummer, and I thought I would try one.

Lady #3: Isn't a hummer a car? How do you go from that to a drink?

Server: (He has become very uncomfortable.) Uh, um, uh, ma'am, do you know what a hummer is?

Lady #4: What do you mean? It's a drink...right?

Server: I suppose... I'll check with the bartender, but a hummer is also a car... and something that...uh, well something that men really enjoy.

Lady #4: Fiddlesticks. I'd like a hummer.

(The server leaves and goes to the bartender.)

Server: You won't believe this, Sally... I need one Sex On the Beach, two chocolate martinis, and um, well, don't get angry—a hummer. Lady at that table says she really needs a hummer.

Bartender: Take your mind out of the gutter! A hummer is a drink born in Detroit that includes rum, Kahlua, ice cream, and some ice, all blended together.

Server: Oh.

As for the other meanings of the term "hummer," check with Cosmopolitan magazine.

New Booze Products: Brilliant and Dumb

Wine and Spirits Daily had two announcements about new spirits products recently. One makes sense and the other—well, you decide.

Good Idea

The flavored whiskey category has been on fire with brands like Wild Turkey American Honey, Jack Daniel's Tennessee Honey, and Jim Beam Red Stag, among others. Now the people from Dewar's Scotch (owned by Bacardi) are entering the flavored whisk(e)y category with Highlander Honey, a scotch infused with honey.

Imagine, they have the audacity to try and break down the stuffiness and out-of-date, sacred walls of the blended scotch category. Never mind the fact that blended scotch growth has been declining or even flattened in the past decade, while other whiskies (including malts) have been growing. It's not about adapting to changing tastes; it's about a stiff upper lip refusing to swallow change.

Check this out. The Diageo head of whisky *outreach* (huh? I think that's a way of saying, "can I buy you a drink?"), was quoted as saying scotch has too much "integrity" and "authenticity" to get into flavors. Also, the Scotch Whiskey Association is not very happy about it. Better to go down with the ship, eh, what?

Hey, it's a good idea for the reasons I shared with *Wine and Spirits Daily*:

"It's a terrific idea and well worth trying," long-time industry exec Arthur Shapiro told WSD." First, the blended scotch market is declining and this could be a shot in the arm. Second, the flavored whiskey (U.S.) brands have "greased the skids" so consumer acceptance would be easier than it might have been before these brands came on the market. Third, it adds contemporariness to the scotch area and removes the stuffiness. Fourth, probably makes for a good mixed drink. Finally, I like the "seriousness" of scotch and the fun of a flavored scotch product."

Put that in your copper still and cook it.

You gotta be kidding me

Pernod Ricard introduced a product that caught my attention.

The company is introducing a line of new products under the Hiram Walker name, called Mama Walker's breakfast liqueurs. Apparently, it's intended to "tap into the comfort food, sweet and savory flavor combinations" trend (or is it a fad?) not to mention the confectionary/cake vodka flavors. This breakfast of champions is available in Maple Bacon, Blueberry Pancake, and Glazed Donut.

Come on—are you serious? Next thing you're going to tell us is that they hardly taste artificial.

Can't you just see the ad campaign?

A bit hung over from a hard night of drinking? Looking for something to smooth out the rough edges? Forget about the all-night diner and the bacon, eggs, and pancake special. Try some of Mama Walker's breakfast liqueurs... we'll perk you right up with our original comfort booze. Just remember... your Mama knows best.

Or:

Tired of the same old breakfast? Cereal, eggs, or fruit can be soooo boring... Start you day off right with Mama Walker's breakfast liqueurs. What a great way to face the stress of what awaits you. Boss on your back? Kids on your nerves? Mama can help. Comes with or without a brown paper bag... But, remember, don't eat breakfast and drive!

Booze Blues

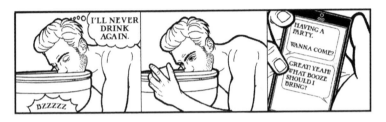

The hangover—lots of interesting ways to describe it. "I have post-party trauma"; "someone slipped me a bad ice cube"; "suffering the wrath of grapes"; "the high cost of low living"; and my favorite, "I was over-served."

No matter how you describe it, overindulgence can be painful the morning after.

First, how does it happen? Aside from the fact that you drank too much (duh), alcohol in large amounts creates a diuretic effect. The body will try to replenish the loss of liquid, often sending a message in the form of dry mouth. According to a researcher at George Mason University, "the body's organs will attempt to replenish their own water, usually stealing water from the brain..." Hence, the headache.

While there doesn't seem to be a surefire cure, there are lots of remedies. They work by providing chemicals your body needs. Eggs, for example, contain cysteine, an amino acid that helps your liver. Potassium, fructose, sodium, and (of course) water are beneficial the next day.

The *Atlantic Wire* has a hangover story that suggests eating a bowl of the Vietnamese soup known as Pho. Some people refer to it as a miracle hangover cure.

Here's an excerpt from Caveday.com, which has lots of information on hangovers:

So how did Pho become nominated as a contender for the best hangover cure? For one, it's a big bowl of soup, so you get uber hydrated. The spices cause you to sweat out all of the toxins and exfoliate the layer of (booze) that has permeated your skin. To add, soup is comfort food. You drink soup when you're sick, and I think that you would agree that you feel sick when you're hungover. Lastly, the main ingredient is magic.

Speaking of Asian remedies, the Japanese suck on Umeboshi, a pickled dried plum/apricot. Apparently it's one of Japan's oldest and best-known hangover cures. The acid raises the pH level easing nausea and stomach pains. The fruit itself provides potassium and sodium.

But it looks like it belongs on the bottom of a toilet bowl. I'd rather give up drinking. Or just stick with bacon and eggs and lots of juice.

Bar in a Bra

The Wine Rack Bra contains a flask, hidden inside with a tube that lets you drink the liquid. It looks like a normal sports bra; but can hold an entire bottle of wine or spirits.

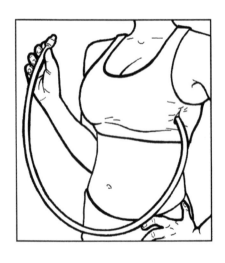

The manufacturer claims the bra has a number of uses. Not only does it allow the wearer to covertly drink the contents, but also in venues where alcohol is sold, you can bring your own less expensive booze and save money. (In this case, I assume that BYOB means Bring Your Own Bra).

The clincher—at least according to ads I've seen online—is that it also serves as a breast enhancement product, allowing the wearer to "turn an A cup into double Ds." But wait; as you drink from a fluid-filled bra, doesn't the breast size get smaller? I guess if you drink enough, you and others won't notice.

You think that's cheesy?

There's a comparable product for men called the Freedom Flask. It's designed to be worn underneath the pants, sitting right in front of the crotch. If that's not disgusting enough, the spigot is located so that you have easy access when you unzip your pants.

So there you have it. American ingenuity in action.

I can't imagine wanting a drink, or wanting to save money badly enough, that I'd use these items.

"Dude... there's weed in my wine"

A story in *The Daily Beast*, was headlined, "Marijuana-Laced Wine Grows More Fashionable in California Wine Country."

Apparently it's quite common for winemakers to produce cannabis cuvées, with bold reds such as Cabernet and Syrah. The recipe is a pound of marijuana dropped into a cask of wine, which yields about 1.5 grams of weed per bottle. The article quotes the president of the Napa Valley Marijuana Growers, who says the combination of alcohol and marijuana produces "an interesting little buzz." "People love wine," he goes on the say, "and they love weed."

I think there are a number of good reasons for marijuana-infused wine to be more readily available.

First, the restaurant industry will benefit, as the amount of food consumed increases, particularly desserts. Second, the wine maven reviews will become more interesting and more fun. As in, "This unpretentious wine, with earthy notes, may have a skunky aroma, but pairs exceptionally well with brownies."

Let's not forget the great naming opportunities, such as Sensimilla Syrah or Ganja Valley Vineyards or even Good Shit Wines.

Mixing alcohol with marijuana reminds me of a Seagram story. While working on new products, the team came up with the idea of flavored tequila called Coyote (see Chapter 3). The flavor was hot peppers, and it was awful. Great name, undrinkable product.

My office at the time was down the corridor from The Glenlivet Tavern, a company-run dining room where executives could have breakfast. On the few occasions when I stopped by, I would always get into trouble. This one thought the market research was wrong, that one thought we needed to be more aggressive in new products. In short, it was a place to avoid.

I slipped up one day, and went in to get a cup of coffee to take back to my desk. I ran into one of the senior executives. He had heard about Coyote's development, and suggested that we consider adding the aroma of cannabis to the product. He thought it would enhance the macho and bad boy aura. I kind of liked the idea, but realized that it couldn't happen. I recall thinking, "No way the TTB approves the liquid. It's a waste of time."

I told him that we would think about it and explore the possibilities. Then we totally ignored the idea. He never asked about it again.

So to all the wine-pot makers out there, I have some experience in this "emerging" category, and will happily share my marketing plans.

Banned Booze

Five Wives Vodka, from Ogden's Own Distillery in Utah, can be sold in that state but not in nearby Idaho. The label has an image of five women, an apparent reference to polygamy.

The Idaho State Liquor Division administrator said the brand is "offensive to a prominent segment of our population and will not be carried." According to *Ad Age*, 25% of the Idaho population is Mormon, compared with 62% in Utah. Leaving that aside, Mormons don't drink—so presumably, they won't be exposed to the product in stores.

The authorities claim that the brand is not being "banned," but was not being listed for marketing reasons. He said the Idaho liquor list has 106 different brands of vodka, and Five Wives "doesn't differentiate itself in any significant way..."

Really? He just described 80% of the vodkas out there. I think it's a clever brand name for a regional product, with lots of marketing opportunities.

In fact, Steve Conlin, marketing director for Ogden's Own, has started selling "Free the Five Wives" t-shirts. He points out that "if you're practicing polygamy, then maybe you're going to be offended...but Mormons are not supposed to be practicing polygamy."

According to Conlin, the designer who came up with the name just liked the idea of five wives sitting around having a drink. (Probably laughing about what a jerk the husband is, among other things).

By the way, a number of beer products that deal directly with polygamy are sold in Idaho. One is Polygamy Pale Ale and the other is Polygamy Porter. The liquor control division points out that they have no jurisdiction over beer. What? You expect consistency from government?

The Marshmallow Booze Made Me Do It...

The Chicago Tribune ran a story about a burglar and an interesting new twist to an old excuse.

Charged with felony burglary (among other related offenses), the gentleman in question broke into a home and stole some property, and so a foot race with police ensued. When he thought he had escaped, he broke into another home—but this time, he lay down on the couch, took off his shoes, and went to sleep. The homeowner found him the next morning and promptly called the police.

He told the police he didn't know how he got there, and the last thing he remembered was drinking marshmallow-flavored vodka.

They should throw the book at him—mainly for his bad taste in booze.

14. Last Call—One for the Road

The following news blurb appeared in *Yahoo News* on August 18, 2000, under the heading *"Diageo and Pernod Ricard to co-bid for Seagram Wine and Spirits."*

The Directors of Diageo have noted recent press speculation concerning Diageo's possible participation in the sale of Seagram's spirits and wine division.

Diageo and Pernod Ricard announce that they have agreed to work together to make an offer for Seagram's wine and spirits business in the forthcoming disposal process.

Diageo does not anticipate making any further announcement until the outcome of its interest in the process is determined.

Once the Bronfman family had decided to sell Seagram—its brands, assets, facilities, properties, and birthright—it wasn't until this date that we learned who the buyers would be.

To avoid anti-trust problems, two sets of buyers "partnered" to take over the company. One team consisted of Brown Forman and Bacardi, and the other was Diageo and Pernod Ricard. It was a fascinating matchup of rival companies, and each of them reflected their own corporate cultures.

The Brown Forman and Bacardi team were the nicest and most professional group of executives. During the due diligence process (of which I was a part, on the Seagram side), the people from these companies went out of their way to commiserate with us and empathize with what we were going through. Brown Forman couldn't buy the whiskey brands because of their prominence in that category, and Bacardi couldn't buy the rums for the same reason. Together, they would carve the company up and avoid any anti-trust actions. Despite years of rivalry and competitive challenges, there was much mutual respect among all the executives. They behaved professionally and decently. Most of us were rooting for them to win.

The other team (Diageo and Pernod Ricard) was another matter.

I felt that the Pernod group was, quite frankly, in over its head. Up to that point, the company was far from a global leader, which is precisely why it went after Seagram. They wanted the scotch (Chivas and Glenlivet),

Seagram Gin, Martell, Mumm, and other smaller brands. Diageo, on the other hand, wanted Chateau and Estates Wine, Crown Royal and Captain Morgan, the two powerhouse brands from Seagram's portfolio.

At the time, I remember thinking that Pernod got the worse end of the deal. For anti-trust or whatever reasons, Diageo got the gems and Pernod got the crumbs. But while the Pernod people looked to me during the meetings like deer caught in the headlights, they were nice enough. They didn't relate to the Seagram people on an empathetic or collegial level, but were more in awe of us. I think those involved at the time were in as much shock as we were. When the dust settled, they would go from a sleepy second-tier company to a player in the global arena. In fact, not long after the Seagram acquisition, Pernod Ricard also bought the Allied Domecq brands (Malibu, Kahlua, and others).

The Diageo people were a different story. The CEO at the time was obnoxious, arrogant, and rude. He behaved offensively throughout the process, like a vindictive conquering general. Witnessing his behavior and the behavior of his colleagues in the meetings convinced me that I'd rather live in an empty refrigerator box than work for Diageo.

In the end, Diageo and Pernod won the day. But I suppose, the old adage "payback is a bitch" prevailed. The Diageo CEO was replaced not long after the acquisition. While the company managed to continue the growth for a while, Crown Royal and Captain Morgan, as of this writing, are experiencing ups and downs. Pernod, on the other hand, has become a world-class player in the alcohol industry; and I, for one, look forward to the day when they surpass Diageo as the global leader.

*   *   *

Roughly a year and a half after the *Yahoo News* release, Seagram closed. For me, that year and a half consisted of a mixture of sadness and joy.

At one extreme, I had the time of my life. First, there were a series of "stay bonuses" (rewards for not leaving), and as the final closing date kept getting pushed back, the bonuses increased in frequency and amount. I had decided that I would leave the corporate world, so collecting checks was a nice sojourn. Moreover, I planned to return to the marketing consulting world and start a practice with my daughter Michelle, so she launched the business while I waited for the end.

Working in a corporate "no man's land" was the closest thing to an extended free lunch I ever had. For example, the sales incentive trip to Paris at the end was unbelievable. I wrote earlier about the Seagram trips and how over-the-top they were; but this was beyond anything we had seen before. While the closing was going on, it was our role to keep the business going and make the numbers promised to the new buyers. We did, and the incentive trip was a well-earned reward. I won't bore you with the details, but suffice it to say that the last night's banquet was at the Palace of Versailles, in the hall of mirrors; we had a 7-course meal served by servers in period costumes, and it ended with cognac and cigars amidst fireworks over the reflecting pool. At the time, I was in charge of distributor and customer relations (among other areas), and this trip was my and everyone else's swan song. My instructions were, since this was "The Last Tango in Paris" (one of my favorite Jimmy Buffett songs), to "spare no expense." As a good corporate soldier, that's exactly what I did.

Nevertheless, the sadness was extreme and pervasive among all the toilers in the vineyard. For more than a year, employees did not know where they would end up. Would Diageo hire them? Pernod? Would they end up staying in the industry or move into unchartered waters? The Seagram management and executives were most sympathetic, and we did what we could to counsel people, get outplacement services, contact headhunters, and anything else to help get everyone placed. We held offsite meetings, which hosted various speakers and experts available for giving advice, including Dick Bolles, author of the best seller, *What Color Is Your Parachute.*

In particular, I felt awful for those whose entire work life had been at Seagram. Many of them were in their late 40's or 50's, and they had nothing but alcohol industry employment in a time of massive consolidation and scarce jobs. Several were in shock, and even seminars based on the best-selling book, *Who Moved My Cheese,* were of little comfort.

While I have no statistics to back me up, I believe that the vast majority (perhaps all) of displaced Seagram alumni and alumnae ended up okay. At least, I hope they did.

⁕   ⁕   ⁕

As for me, when the lights went out, I decided that I would not consult with any companies in the alcohol industry. It didn't take long, however, to learn that the knowledge I had acquired at Seagram and the **Booze Business** over 15 years was—well, low-hanging fruit for a startup practice. My own protestations to the contrary, AM Shapiro and Associates worked with a wide range of companies in different industries, but the alcohol industry paid most of the bills.

In fact, by the time my daughter and partner left to raise a family, we had consulted with a lot of alcohol companies. I looked at this as a kind of "fellowship" in the business, whereby I learned more about the overall industry than I had at Seagram. Ultimately, startup ventures caught my interest, and writing—both generally, and about the **Booze Business** in particular—has become my work life passion.

* * *

"Changes In Latitudes, Changes In Attitudes"
By Jimmy Buffett

[Chorus]
It's those changes in latitudes,
changes in attitudes nothing remains quite the same.
With all of our running and all of our cunning,
If we couldn't laugh, we would all go insane.

Reading departure signs in some big airport
Reminds me of the places I've been.
Visions of good times that brought so much pleasure
Makes me want to go back again.
If it suddenly ended tomorrow,
I could somehow adjust to the fall.
Good times and riches and son of a bitches,
I've seen more than I can recall

Changes in Latitudes, Changes In Attitudes (Jimmy Buffett)

©2005 Coral Reefer Music (BMI)

ALL RIGHTS RESERVED. USED BY PERMISSION.

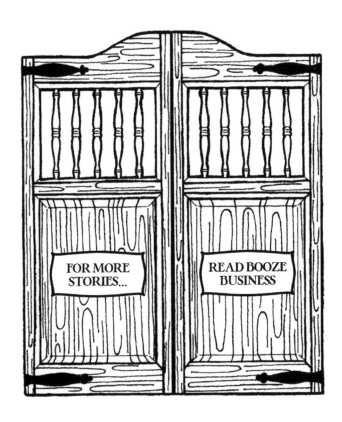

ACKNOWLEDGMENTS AND THANKS

Any journey of this sort takes, time, patience, and the support of friends and family. Two observers of the writing process and creativity who I follow closely are Seth Godin and Steven Pressfield. Both of them write about Resistance and how to overcome it. Here's how they both describe it:

The resistance is the voice in the back of our head telling us to back off, be careful, go slow, compromise. The resistance is writer's block and putting jitters and every project that ever shipped late because people couldn't stay on the same page long enough to get something out the door.

This book would not have happened if it were not for the encouragement of my family, and their help to overcome the resistance. Thank you to my darling wife Marlene, for your endless willingness to edit my posts and help me to sharpen my thinking. To my daughter and former partner, Michelle, for her encouragement. And to my older daughter, Mindy, who tirelessly read multiple drafts, provided incredible insights, and made significant contributions to the narrative.

To all my friends and colleagues for their willingness to read the manuscript along the way, and help sharpen its focus. People like James Espey, Jett Yang, Bill Berenter, Byron Hoover, Steve Bellini, Michael Schwab, and Eileen Higgins, who went beyond the call of duty and helped whip the book into shape. A special thank you to my friend, Jackie Summers, who you met a number of times in this book and is my trusted sounding board and good friend.

I am especially grateful to those who took the time and effort to read the manuscript and provide their thoughts on the book. Thank you Mark Brown, Emily Pennington, Elwyn Gladstone, and Richard Lewis.

Thank you Hannah Forman for your guidance with this book—the text, graphics, and other aspects of the process. Thank you as well for teaching me about the digital world and marketing. Without you, the blog would be second-rate, and this book may never have come about. Thank you also for the team you put into place including bringing Miki Hickel on board for this project. Miki is a talented artist whose illustrations grace these pages. She also designed the cover, layout and index of the book. To Anya Jaremko-Greenwold, a world-class editor, whom I hope to work with again.

ARTHUR SHAPIRO

\#   \#   \#   \#

ABOUT THE AUTHOR

My work life began in consumer and market research, working for a public opinion polling company called Yankelovich, Skelly and White. In the early 1980's, I started my own marketing consulting company in conjunction with United Press International. That business was folded into the Roper Organization so I was back to market research and polling.

Along the way I got an MBA from Fordham. In 2005, I taught two course there– one on marketing and one on market research.

I joined the Seagram Spirits and Wine Company in 1986 as Vice President Marketing Research. What followed was a number of different marketing assignments in the US and globally including Vice President New Products, Senior Vice President Marketing Asia/Pacific/Global Duty Free, Global Head of Marketing Services and my longest position, Executive Vice President Marketing for the Americas. The United States marketing job at Seagram was somewhat high profile and I was fortunate enough to be chosen to the Ad Age Power 50 and Marketing 100. I spent 15 years at Seagram and 10 of them were as head of US marketing. My "15 minutes of fame" came when I led the effort by Seagram to end the voluntary ban on broadcast advertising in 1993.

Seagram closed in 2002 and I started a marketing consulting company together with my daughter Michelle. The company, A|M Shapiro & Associates, continues even though Michelle left to live in California and raise a family. The consulting work is partly in the spirits business and partly in general consumer-marketing areas.

In the alcohol space, my clients have included many of the large companies and a range of others in startup modes. In fact, my consulting practice these days is limited to startup ventures, where I provide marketing advice in brand strategy, consumer insights, and integrated communications.

I like to describe myself as a part time marketing and business consultant with a full time passion for telling stories through my blog, plays, and film.

My blog, **Booze Business** (http://boozebusiness.com) is dedicated to the spirits, wine and beer industries. Despite its size and growth, the alcohol industry is small. It's a business of people, relationships and stories. Stories that I love to tell. You've read many of them in this book.

I've been writing plays for the past six years. One of my short plays, *Stuck*, won a short play festival in the 2011 Short Play Festival at Players Theatre in New York City. A full-length play, *Brooklyn Moonshine War*, had a staged reading in 2013 at the Midtown International Film Festival. It is a full-length play based on the actual "invasion" of Brooklyn by Federal Marshals, tax collectors and 1,200 US Army troops in 1870.

More recently, I have turned my attention toward filmmaking and screenwriting. Together with some very talented filmmakers, we have formed **Warwick Street Productions LLC** and plan to produce a range of films. Our first production, **Bereavement**, is a short film starring Mark Linn-Baker. Bereavement has been selected into six festivals including the LA International Short Film festival, and the Chesapeake Bay Film Festival. We have also completed a web series called **The Mentors**, created by my partner, **Lauren Ashley Carter** and written by and featuring **Lewis Black**.

Finally, I've combined passions and **Warwick Street Productions** is telling stories through branded content (also known as branded entertainment) and there are many projects on the drawing board and in production. Basically, and as I mentioned in Chapter 4, branded content is a story that is told and made with a brand's personality, positioning and marketing objectives in mind.

To me it's the best of both my worlds.

Many thanks for reading, and if you want to contact me to say hi or even tell me about the new alcohol product you're working on, feel free to write me at: arthur@boozebusiness.com or a.shapiro@mac.com

You can also find me at https://www.facebook.com/boozebusiness

LinkedIn: https://www.linkedin.com/in/arthur-shapiro-130294

My website: http://www.amshapiro.com

INDEX

Made in the USA
Middletown, DE
02 November 2016